WTC VIEW
BY BRIAN SLOAN

DRAMATISTS
PLAY SERVICE
INC.

WTC VIEW
Copyright © 2012, Brian Sloan

All Rights Reserved

CAUTION: Professionals and amateurs are hereby warned that performance of WTC VIEW is subject to payment of a royalty. It is fully protected under the copyright laws of the United States of America, and of all countries covered by the International Copyright Union (including the Dominion of Canada and the rest of the British Commonwealth), and of all countries covered by the Pan-American Copyright Convention, the Universal Copyright Convention, the Berne Convention, and of all countries with which the United States has reciprocal copyright relations. All rights, including without limitation professional/amateur stage rights, motion picture, recitation, lecturing, public reading, radio broadcasting, television, video or sound recording, all other forms of mechanical, electronic and digital reproduction, transmission and distribution, such as CD, DVD, the Internet, private and file-sharing networks, information storage and retrieval systems, photocopying, and the rights of translation into foreign languages are strictly reserved. Particular emphasis is placed upon the matter of readings, permission for which must be secured from the Author's agent in writing.

The English language stock and amateur stage performance rights in the United States, its territories, possessions and Canada for WTC VIEW are controlled exclusively by DRAMATISTS PLAY SERVICE, INC., 440 Park Avenue South, New York, NY 10016. No professional or nonprofessional performance of the Play may be given without obtaining in advance the written permission of DRAMATISTS PLAY SERVICE, INC., and paying the requisite fee.

Inquiries concerning all other rights should be addressed to Abrams Artists Agency, 275 Seventh Avenue, 26th Floor, New York, NY 10001. Attn: Peter Hagan.

SPECIAL NOTE
Anyone receiving permission to produce WTC VIEW is required to give credit to the Author as sole and exclusive Author of the Play on the title page of all programs distributed in connection with performances of the Play and in all instances in which the title of the Play appears for purposes of advertising, publicizing or otherwise exploiting the Play and/or a production thereof. The name of the Author must appear on a separate line, in which no other name appears, immediately beneath the title and in size of type equal to 50% of the size of the largest, most prominent letter used for the title of the Play. No person, firm or entity may receive credit larger or more prominent than that accorded the Author.

SPECIAL NOTE ON SONGS AND RECORDINGS
For performances of copyrighted songs, arrangements or recordings mentioned in this Play, the permission of the copyright owner(s) must be obtained. Other songs, arrangements or recordings may be substituted provided permission from the copyright owner(s) of such songs, arrangements or recordings is obtained; or songs, arrangements or recordings in the public domain may be substituted.

AUTHOR'S NOTE

GENERAL

The most important thing to keep in mind when putting together a production of this challenging show is that WTC VIEW is not a funeral. It is a play about a guy trying to find a roommate in New York City. Eric's roommate ad is what sets the action of the play in motion, and that's what keeps the play moving forward until its final scene. Granted, all of the action is taking place during an extraordinary time in the city's history: the aftermath of the 9/11 attacks.

My intention in writing this play was to show what life was really like in New York City during this unusual time. There was sadness, of course. But there were many other emotions going on, too. People were living their lives in the shadow of this immense tragedy with a mixture of perseverance, fear, humor, shock, excitement, and sorrow. So it is essential that the actors working on WTC VIEW play all these conflicting emotions and, in general, do not treat the material too reverently. It is not a eulogy for the dead but rather a declaration from the living.

NOTE FOR ACTORS

Every scene in WTC VIEW is ultimately is about one thing: Eric has to get a roommate. That's why people are coming to visit him — they are there to see the apartment. It's even why Josie is coming to visit as well — to help move this process along. No one who comes to see the apartment is there to look out the window, though many of them do. They are not there to mourn, though this happens as well. The reason that they have all been brought to this place is to find a room in Manhattan. For all of them, this is an urgent need. Everyone in this play is essentially homeless and looking for a place to live, some more desperately than others. As long as this simple fact is not forgotten, the play will go well. However, the minute actors forget this, the whole exercise will fall apart.

METROPOLITAN COLLEGE OF
LIBRARY, 12TH FLOOR
431 CANAL STREET
NEW YORK, NY 10013

HUMOR

WTC VIEW has a lot of humor in it. This may be surprising to some readers, but it is not surprising to anyone who lived in New York during that awful period, especially those living downtown. Humor was the only way to keep one's sanity in the face of such an immense tragedy. Thus, the humor in this play is essential to making the show work. It was included intentionally, so please do not ignore it or think it may be in bad taste. It is not. It is, however, the magical key for keeping the audience with you as they take the difficult and intense journey that the play requires. So whenever the actors find a moment of humor, they should take it. It will keep the play moving, and it will keep the audience from being overwhelmed by a subject that is, by its nature, overwhelming.

PACING

There is a lot of dialogue in this play, and there is no intermission. Thus, the pacing is another essential element to making the show run well. This is New York City and people talk fast. There is a danger in actors seeking out meaningful pauses in every line due to the sensitive subject matter. Some pauses are justified and are often indicated in the script. Otherwise, pauses should be avoided as much as possible. When it comes to the play's monologues, it is extremely important to remember that this is not Shakespeare; the monologues are not speeches but stories being told by one person to another. They should not be addressed to the audience and should not be declamatory. They are simply stories that one character is relating to another. Some of them are intense, some of them are funny, but all of them should be told in as conversational and natural a style as possible.

ALEX'S MONOLOGUE

The previous note about monologues goes double for Alex. The story of his escape from the Trade Center is a memorable one and, in some ways, is seen as the centerpiece of the play. It is also a story that Alex knows very well It is not the first time he is telling it, since people have been asking him about his extraordinary tale of survival for more than three weeks. This does not mean he is not affected by it. But every word ... should ... not ... be ... emphasized.

There are, of course, some phrases and moments that should be, like his realization that the blood on his pants is not his own. But this monologue should be just like his escape: fast and miraculous. Also, for those wondering, Alex's monologue is not based on any one survivor's story. It is a compilation and composite of multiple tales of survival at the World Trade Center on that fateful morning. Some people were terribly injured on the elevators, but others were not. Despite the debris and bodies falling, some people escaped unscathed from the plaza and some did not. Many thousands of people were incredibly lucky that day. And of course, nearly three thousand people were not.

ERIC
Eric is a gay man. But even more importantly, he is in the classic sense the Everyman of this play. Eric is a character who is on stage throughout the entire show, and the audience must be able to identify with him and go with him on this difficult journey. It is essential to cast an actor who is likeable and has the ability to keep the audience with him throughout the show. In terms of type, even though Eric is a gay man living in New York, he is atypical and should not be cast nor played like a character in a sitcom about a gay man living in New York. His sexuality is a part of the story but it is not THE story of this play. As for Joey from Rainbow Roommates, that's a whole different story.

MESSAGES
The answering machine messages that open the show are tricky. There is a tendency to read them with the hindsight of history and overdo the emotions in them. It's very important to keep the tone conversational, especially with Will's first message. He does not know exactly what he is witnessing and he should sound more puzzled than horrified. Also, since this is the first line of the play, it should set the tone for the show and that tone is not hysterical or panicked or the voice of a TV news reporter doing a standup on the Brooklyn Bridge. It's just a guy driving his car to work who sees something strange that he cannot understand.

HISTORICAL NOTES

My inspiration in writing this play was to provide an historical snapshot of life in New York during September 2001. These are some historical notes which further explain unusual situations, names and places mentioned in WTC VIEW. I strongly encourage actors cast in this show to do some research on their own about what life was like for New Yorkers on and after 9/11. A great starting point is local publications, like *The New Yorker* and *New York* magazine and, of course, *The New York Times*. But below are some of the basics that can help actors in their understanding of the play and some of its unique language and situations.

AIR PATROLS

For more than six months after 9/11, twenty-four hour combat patrols of F-15 and F-16 aircraft circled the skies above New York City. They generally flew unnoticed at high altitudes but, occasionally and without explanation, the jets would zoom lower and create a lot of noise and vibration on the ground. These air patrols were the first of their kind over the United States since the Cuban Missile Crisis in 1962.

CENTURY 21

Century 21 is a family-owned department store in Lower Manhattan that, since 1961, has been doing a brisk business selling designer clothes and brand-name items at 25–75% discounts. It's popular with New Yorkers but is often jammed with foreign tourists as well. The store is located on Church Street between Cortlandt and Fulton Streets, directly across from the World Trade Center. The store survived the collapse of Towers 1, 2 and 7 yet did suffer major internal damage and was closed after 9/11. It reopened to the public in March 2002.

UNION SQUARE

On the afternoon of 9/11, students from New York University who lived in dorms near Union Square (14th Street and Broadway) started congregating on the steps on the south side of the park when all their classes were cancelled. They lit candles, sang songs, and wrote statements of mourning and pleas for peace using chalk on the park's dark paving stones. When city officials closed off Manhattan south of 14th Street to non-residents that night, people from all over the city came to the Square, as it was the closest people could get to Lower Manhattan. These gatherings lasted for nearly a week.

800 NUMBER

In the weeks following 9/11, advertisements began to appear on TV, radio and public transportation for 1-800-LIFENET. This number was set up as part of a larger initiative entitled Project Liberty, sponsored by the FEMA and the Center for Mental Health Services. Its purpose was to provide free crisis counseling and mental health support services to individuals in the Tri-State area who were affected, directly or indirectly, by the attacks.

MAYORAL ELECTION

September 11, 2001 was the Democratic primary in the race for Mayor of New York City. Polling places opened that morning, but after the attacks on the World Trade Center, most of them were shut down by the afternoon and the city rescheduled the primary for later that month. That rescheduled election was so close that there was a run-off in October between Mark Green and Bronx Borough President Fernando Ferrer. Green, previously the city's Public Advocate, won and was the Democratic candidate for mayor against Michael Bloomberg, a Republican. When Bloomberg was endorsed by Mayor Giuliani, a national hero at that point, the race shifted in his favor and Bloomberg won by 3 percentage points.

WTC VIEW was first presented by Us Productions as part of the New York International Fringe Festival (Elena K. Holy, Producing Artistic Director) at The Bottle Factory Theatre in New York City on August 11, 2003. It was produced by Helena Webb and directed by Andrew Volkoff; the sound design was by Jim Van Bergen; and the stage manager was Cynthia Ann Thomas. The cast was as follows:

ERIC	Michael Urie
JEREMY	Jeremy Beazlie
JOSIE	Elizabeth Kapplow
KEVIN	Lucas Papaelias
JEFF	Michael Linstroth
ALEX	Nick Potenzieri
MAX	Jay Gillespie
WILL	Jason Dietz
VICTOR	M. Rosenthal
JOEY	Kevin Ray
CARLOS	Lucas Papaelias
LORENZO	Mark Sam

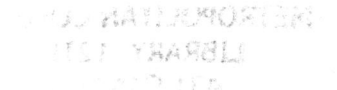

WTC VIEW received its Off-Broadway premiere at 59E59 Theaters (Elysabeth Kleinhans, President & Artistic Director) in New York City, on May 19, 2011. It was produced by Brian Sloan and directed by Andrew Volkoff; the set design was by Brian Prather; the costume design was by Jacob A. Climer; the lighting design was by Jeff Davis; the sound design was by David M. Lawson; the stage manager was Carol Sullivan; and the company manager was George Heslin. The cast was as follows:

ERIC	Nick Lewis
JEREMY	Bob Braswell
JOSIE	Leah Curney
KEVIN	Michael Carlsen
JEFF	Torsten Hillhouse
ALEX	Patrick Edward O'Brien
MAX	Martin Edward Cohen
WILL	Jay Gaussoin
VICTOR	Brian Prather
JOEY	Chad Miller
CARLOS	Jorge Cordova
LORENZO	Nick Potenzieri

CHARACTERS

ERIC, 33, a boyish freelance photographer

JEREMY, 26, a charming and proper Brit

JOSIE, 33, a stylish Upper East Side wife

KEVIN, 27, a strung-out chain smoker

JEFF, 37, a jocky political consultant

ALEX, 29, a cute Wall Street guy

MAX, 20, a peacenik NYU student

WILL, 38, the ex-boyfriend (voice)

VICTOR, 28, the politely chatty Southerner (voice)

JOEY, 22, the hyper chorus boy (voice)

CARLOS, 49, the Latino landlord (voice)

LORENZO, 30, the heavily-accented Italian import (voice)

PLACE

The play's action takes place in an empty bedroom of a two-bedroom tenement apartment in SoHo, New York City.

TIME

After a short prologue, the play is set during the last week of September 2001.

The play is performed without an intermission.

TIMELINE

Tuesday 9/11 (Prologue messages)

Tuesday 9/11 – Wednesday 9/20 (Eric stays in Brooklyn)

Saturday 9/22 (Eric packing Stephen's stuff)

Sunday 9/23 (Moving Stephen's stuff out)

Scene 1 — Monday 9/24 — afternoon (Jeremy)

Scene 2 — Monday 9/24 — night (Josie)

Scene 3 — Tuesday 9/25 — afternoon (Kevin)

Scene 4 — Wednesday 9/26 — afternoon (Jeff)

Scene 5 — Thursday 9/27 — night (Josie)

Scene 6 — Friday 9/28 — past midnight (Alex)

Scene 7 — Friday 9/28 — early that morning (Alex)

Scene 8 — Friday 9/28 — afternoon (Max)

Friday 9/28 – 10/1 (Eric back in Brooklyn)

Scene 9 — Monday 10/1 — late afternoon (Josie)

WTC VIEW

Prologue

The stage is dark. On the stage left, a bare window is illuminated from behind by a vague morning light, with a small American flag Scotch-taped to the sash. It is the kind a child might wave at a parade. The sound of sirens are heard ... first one, then a couple, then many more, overlapping and creating a cacophony of emergency sounds. A computerized answering machine voice comes on.

ANSWERING MACHINE. Tuesday, 8:49 A.M.
WILL. *(Voiceover.)* Hey — it's me. I'm taking the car into Manhattan today — easier than finding a space to park. Anyway, I'm on the Brooklyn Bridge and there's a huge ... fire on ... in the, uh, one of the towers of the World Trade Center. It must encompass, I don't know, fifteen floors. Smoke billowing out, coming out of the windows. It's ... oh man. It's enormous, it's amaze — just look out your window Eric. Bye.
ANSWERING MACHINE. Tuesday, 11:32 A.M.
JOSIE. *(Voiceover.)* Hey Eric — where are you? It's Josie. Just making a round of downtown calls. I hope you're well and I hope you're safe. I don't know where you are today but maybe not being home is safer since you're so close. Anyway, I'm getting hysterical and I'm sure you're fine and I'll talk to you soon ... I hope.
ANSWERING MACHINE. Tuesday, 4:12 P.M.
WILL. *(Voiceover.)* Eric — Eric — are you there? Pick up the phone. Oh my god — I've been trying to get through to you all afternoon. I really would love it if you could call me back. You can try my work number uptown. Or my cell which I've been carrying

with me since this happened. I'm worried because Sharon's okay, Tom's okay ... but you're the hardest to get in touch with downtown. All the circuits kept saying they're busy. So I'm a little — I just wanna be sure you're okay, Eric, because — *(Voice catching.)* Alright, I'm gonna try and not get emotional here. But ... *(getting emotional.)* OK — just call me. *(The sirens fade out. The light in the window goes out. The stage is black.)*

Scene 1

Lights up on an empty apartment bedroom. At the center of the stage, 3 cardboard boxes are packed and taped closed. Near them is one box that is open and brimming with stuff. Next to the window at stage left is a very old air conditioner, with a can of air freshener on top of it. At stage right, is a dresser with an alarm clock and an answering machine on top. Next to the dresser, is a door that leads to the rest of the apartment.

From the doorway at stage right, a young man, in his early 30s, enters the room wearing a thrift store T-shirt, old jeans and a pair of new sneakers. He is unshaven and smoking a cigarette. He looks at the boxes on the floor and moves them around, trying to arrange them to look nicer as if that's possible. He goes to the window and opens it. A breeze comes in which he enjoys for a second. Then, making a face, he quickly closes it again. Coughing, he reaches for the can of air freshener on top of the A/C unit and gives the room a thorough misting.

ANSWERING MACHINE. Wednesday, 10:31 A.M.
JEREMY. *(Voiceover. British accent.)* Hullo — I'm ringing about the advert in yesterday's *Village Voice*. For the two-bedroom share. I'm hoping it's still available as I desperately need a flat. I know it's a dreadful time but if you could give me a ring I'd be very grateful. I'm at the St. Regis Hotel ... 753-4500. Name's Jeremy Thornton. Thanks so much. *(After putting the air freshener back down, the man*

walks over to the window, almost in a trance, staring out. Suddenly, the jarring buzz of a New York City door buzzer goes off, sounding like an electrocution. The man jumps accordingly and then opens the window quickly and tosses his cigarette out, trying to clear the air too before closing it again. He walks over to a door at stage right, opens it and hits a button offstage.)
MAN. *(Offstage.)* Yeah …
JEREMY. *(Offstage.)* Hullo — it's Jeremy. *(He buzzes him in. Then, he looks around the room, still trying to fix things up. He tries in vain to clear the air. There is knocking heard offstage. The man rushes out of the room and disappears offstage.)*
JEREMY. *(Offstage.)* Sorry I'm so terribly late.
MAN. *(Offstage.)* You have trouble finding it? *(The man reenters with Jeremy, a young but proper Londoner, dressed in a smart V-neck sweater with a matching tie.)*
JEREMY. A bit. I went uptown when I thought I was going downtown. I still don't know my way round.
MAN. Ah — just moved here?
JEREMY. September 7th.
MAN. Oh no.
JEREMY. Oh yes.
MAN. Well … it can only get better right? *(Jeremy smiles wanly, as the man laughs a bit too nervously.)*
JEREMY. So this is the room you're letting?
MAN. Oh — yeah. This is the bedroom. And, uh, the kitchen and bath are back — *(Jeremy pulls out a small notepad and a pen and takes notes.)*
JEREMY. Sorry — what was the rent again?
MAN. Twelve hundred a month. Utilities included. *(A beat.)* So you're here for work?
JEREMY. I'm assisting the concierge at the St. Regis Hotel.
MAN. Very classy …
JEREMY. And you said it was non-smoking, is that right?
MAN. Yeah. Technically. I quit this summer.
JEREMY. *(Smelling skeptically.)* I see …
MAN. It's just — a friend was over. My neighbor. My smoking neighbor … always, you know, smoking up the joint. *(An awkward beat as Jeremy looks around the room judgmentally.)*
MAN. Uh — I'm sorry I took so long to get back to you.
JEREMY. Oh — it's quite alright.

MAN. Things were a little ... crazy down here.
JEREMY. Actually, I feel just awful about calling like that.
MAN. Like what?
JEREMY. Ringing you the day after the 11th. You must've thought I was mad.
MAN. Not really.
JEREMY. No?
MAN. I had nine messages about the apartment that day.
JEREMY. You're joking.
MAN. Oh no. Yours was pretty tame actually. Some of the messages were unbelievable. This one guy was like — "Yeah, I wanna come down and see it this afternoon." I mean, unless he was in the National Guard ...
JEREMY. Still — I must apologize for calling like that. I don't know what I was thinking.
MAN. I don't think anyone knew what they were thinking. *(There is an awkward pause as Jeremy looks at the man, troubled.)*
JEREMY. I'm sorry. I forgot your name?
ERIC. Oh — Eric.
JEREMY. Eric. Right. Of course. With all the calls I've been making ...
ERIC. It can get confusing. Especially these days ...
JEREMY. May I ask you how long you've been here, Eric?
ERIC. Uh — sure. Hmmmm ... let me see ... about nine years. Wow. *(Semi-amazed.)* Nine years. Almost ten ...
JEREMY. You must like it very much then?
ERIC. Kinda. I ... I got the apartment when I was in school and it was dirt cheap and so I just kinda stayed.
JEREMY. And your roommate's moved out?
ERIC. Oh ... yeah. He's gone. Got his stuff out yesterday. Most of it ... *(They spy the dresser.)* My ex is coming to get that later.
JEREMY. And that was your roommate?
ERIC. No — the ex wasn't the roommate. Kinda why he's the ex.
JEREMY. Pardon.
ERIC. Wanted me to move in with him.
JEREMY. Ah — how long were you together?
ERIC. He only lived here a few months.
JEREMY. Sorry — I meant you and your ex.
ERIC. Oh — uh, almost two years.
JEREMY. Oh — I'm sorry then.

ERIC. Don't be. You wouldn't be looking at this if I'd moved in.
JEREMY. Quite true.
ERIC. Have you seen a lot of apartments?
JEREMY. This is actually the first.
ERIC. Wow. You were the first to call.
JEREMY. *(Shocked.)* Oh! Now that makes me feel wonderful. I was the very first!? That's absolutely ghoulish.
ERIC. Ghoulish?
JEREMY. Eh, morbid. You know ...
ERIC. Sure. It's just you don't hear the word very often — ghoulish.
JEREMY. When I left that message, I was at my wits end. You see, I've been living at the St. Regis since I arrived.
ERIC. Doesn't sound so bad ...
JEREMY. One would think ... except when you're being shuffled around to a different hotel room every night it can be somewhat — disconcerting. Then when the planes got grounded, all the guests were stuck at the hotel and there weren't any rooms. And the staff couldn't get home because of all the transport issues. So they decided to lodge us in the ballroom the night of the 11th ... on cots! Like some high-class vagabond shelter. Dreadful. And that was my last straw. So when I called I was just —
ERIC. You don't have to apologize. I don't think calling about the ad was ... uh ... what's that word ...
JEREMY. Ghoulish?
ERIC. *(Smiling cause he just wanted to hear it again.)* Right. I don't think you're "ghoulish" at all. *(Jeremy smiles appreciatively, to know he's not so improper. Jeremy goes to look out the window. Eric looks around the room nervously.)*
JEREMY. Lots of sun. Nice view. *(A beat.)* Could you see them from here?
ERIC. Oh yeah. Right at the end of the street. Huge.
JEREMY. You weren't here when —
ERIC. *(Wearily.)* Saw the whole thing out the window.
JEREMY. *(Taken aback.)* Good god — it must have been horrific for you.
ERIC. *(Startled by Jeremy's reaction.)* Yeah. It was, you know. *(Change of subject.)* Uh ... where were you?
JEREMY. I was at work. My third day. Unbelievable.
ERIC. Literally. I still can't believe it. In the morning, I have that

instant right when I wake up where I forget the whole thing and then I remember it and it's just — unbelievable.

JEREMY. But being here ... you're so close. It must have been terrifying.

ERIC. It was pretty bad ...

JEREMY. How far from —

ERIC. I don't know ... about 12 blocks.

JEREMY. Was there any ...

ERIC. No — strangely enough. The wind blew most of that stuff towards Brooklyn.

JEREMY. Poor Brooklyn ... *(Jeremy is now staring out the window, lost in thought. Eric would like to move this along.)*

ERIC. So — whattya think of the place?

JEREMY. It's lovely. When do you need someone?

MAN. I was supposed to get someone in here on the 15th of September but ... well, that didn't happen. The landlord let the situation slide a bit because of everything that was going on. But I definitely need someone here for October.

JEREMY. So ... how should we proceed then?

ERIC. Let's see — I'm planning to decide by the end of the week, the 28th, so someone can move in on the weekend.

JEREMY. I like it a lot but it is the first place I've seen ...

ERIC. Why don't you give me a call tomorrow if you're interested and we can take it from there.

JEREMY. Splendid. And I'll ring you either way. I don't want to leave you guessing.

ERIC. *(Surprised.)* Wow. That's nice.

JEREMY. It's only the proper thing to do.

ERIC. Not if you live in New York.

JEREMY. I'm still new.

ERIC. They used to say you have to be here at least two years before you don't feel like a tourist.

JEREMY. I believe that schedule has been accelerated due to recent events.

ERIC. Yeah — now it'll only take you a year. *(They smile at each other. Jeremy makes his way to leave.)*

JEREMY. Now ... when I get downstairs how do I find "uptown."

ERIC. Oh — when you go out the front door, so you don't get lost, if you look for the Empire State Building, that's uptown. And downtown is ... well ... not.

JEREMY. Right. Well, I'll ring you soon.
ERIC. *(Motioning to leave.)* Great. Let me show you —
JEREMY. I'll see myself out. Take care ... *(Eric shuts the door behind him and smiles to himself, pleased.)*
ERIC. Cheerio.

Scene 2

In darkness, the answering machine is heard.

ANSWERING MACHINE. Monday, 11:23 A.M.
WILL. *(Voiceover.)* Hey — it's me. You left a bunch of clothes from when you were here and, despite my better judgment, I washed them for you. Anyway, let me know when I can come by — as for that dresser, I don't know if I really want it. It sounds ugly. But give me a ring and let me know how you're doing, okay? And if you found a roommate yet. *(Lights up on a stylishly dressed woman, about the same age as Eric, standing at the window with the flag. Josie's back is to the audience as she stands there, very still, staring out the window. The sound of a door opening is heard offstage.)*
ANSWERING MACHINE. Monday, 1:32 P.M.
KEVIN. *(Voiceover.)* What's up? I'm calling about the roommate "situation". I'm looking for a place immediately ... yesterday even. I've only got a cell right now — 917-439-4276. But give me a ring and I'll come check it out. Thanks and peace, man.
ERIC *(Offstage.)* Delivery!
JOSIE. I can't believe it's still smoking. It's been two weeks!
ERIC *(Offstage.)* They're nowhere near putting it all out.
JOSIE. What?!
ERIC *(Offstage.)* The *Times* said it's probably gonna be another month or so. Maybe longer.
JOSIE. Jesus. *(Eric enters the room carrying some paper sacks of take-out food and wearing an industrial type surgical mask. Josie turns away from the window.)*
ERIC. Could be the longest burning industrial fire in the U.S.
JOSIE. *(Re: the mask.)* Don't you think you're overreacting a bit.

ERIC. No.
JOSIE. It's fine. They've been testing.
ERIC. It doesn't smell fine.
JOSIE. But it's not gonna kill you.
ERIC. Look Uptown Girl — I'm breathing this crap every day — 24/7. On top of that, the smell is awful. So technically, if it's not actually toxic, the smell alone is by far enough to make me gag and then choke to death on the take out and then would you think I was overreacting to the air quality deal? *(Josie stands there staring at him, studying him.)*
JOSIE. That was a bit of a rant.
ERIC. You asked me about the mask and I gave you an answer.
JOSIE. Definitely a rant.
ERIC. I'm fine.
JOSIE. Did you call that 800 number?
ERIC. It was busy.
JOSIE. Did you try again?
ERIC. It's busy for a reason. There are thousands of other people much worse off than me because they really need help.
JOSIE. Eric — you went through a major traumatic —
ERIC. The food's getting cold.
JOSIE. You're not listening to me.
ERIC. Actually, I am listening and even comprehending what you're saying because remember last week when you told me I wasn't eating enough so today you came over to check up on me and I picked up tons of Thai food for us to gorge ourselves on so I can get nice and fat the way you like me.
JOSIE. Ranting —
ERIC. *(Indicating bags.)* Eating. *(They both sit down on boxes and Eric arranges the food.)*
JOSIE. I'm glad you're eating a lot but other than that …
ERIC. Things are fine. Oh — I even saw a potential roommate.
JOSIE. That's good. So how was he?
ERIC. He was great.
JOSIE. Yeah? Was he cute?
ERIC. I don't know. I guess. That's not supposed to matter.
JOSIE. It does.
ERIC. Josie — you're not supposed to be attracted to your roommate. It's very bad according to, I dunno, someone …
JOSIE. I'm not saying you should be "attracted" to him and start

sleeping with him or anything dirty.
ERIC. So what are you saying?
JOSIE. Bottom line — you have to look at him. Every day. So it's like buying a nice piece of furniture or a rug. Pick something nice. Something you like.
ERIC. Okay — that was sooo Upper East Side.
JOSIE. Just making an analogy.
ERIC. Alright — He was cute.
JOSIE. Good. Half the battle right there.
ERIC. Oh and he's British which is kinda fun.
JOSIE. British? Oh — I don't know …
ERIC. *(With an accent.)* He was being awfully clever and saying the most smashing things.
JOSIE. Did you flirt with him?
ERIC. Uh — I'm pretty sure he was straight.
JOSIE. I thought you said he was British.
ERIC. Gay or straight or whatever — I don't need to be flirting my way back into another dysfunctional relationship.
JOSIE. Don't worry. You'll find someone. The right someone this time.
ERIC. You always say that.
JOSIE. I found someone.
ERIC. And you always say that.
JOSIE. Remember all those horrible guys I went through in my 20s.
ERIC. *(With British accent.)* Quite vividly, yes.
JOSIE. And Will was what, you're first serious, semi-committed —
ERIC. Semi? What do you mean semi?
JOSIE. You never moved in. That's semi.
ERIC. You don't have to move in with someone to be committed.
JOSIE. Apparently, you do with Will.
ERIC. Nice.
JOSIE. The point is you gave it a shot, you guys were together for over two years and you learned a lot. A nice test run.
ERIC. Test run?! If Will could hear you —
JOSIE. And now you're ready for the real thing.
ERIC. Wait-wait-wait a minute. I remember having a conversation with you back in July when you were saying that Will was the real thing.
JOSIE. What can I say — he was until he wasn't.
ERIC. Have you thought about starting an advice column?

JOSIE. This is so you, Eric. To be arguing over the past. I mean, it's over, okay. Will is in the past. Gone. It's a whole new world now.
ERIC. Ergo the mask.
JOSIE. I'm talking about you here.
ERIC. I know.
JOSIE. Really?
ERIC. I. Know.
JOSIE. Good. Now pass me a spring roll. I'm starving. *(He passes the spring roll. Eric gets up and, with his back to Josie, pulls his pack of cigarettes from the dresser drawer.)* What are you doing?
ERIC. Quitting smoking next year.
JOSIE. Eric —
ERIC. This is only my first one of the day.
JOSIE. You said you were eating.
ERIC. I will. Just after this.
JOSIE. Great. Can you open the window at least?
ERIC. Are you kidding?
JOSIE. No — you're smoking and I'm trying to eat.
ERIC. The air is awful today.
JOSIE. Then open the window and put your mask on.
ERIC. I can't smoke with my mask on.
JOSIE. Okay — you realize how absurd this is getting?
ERIC. I'll open it a crack. *(He does. Eric reacts to the smell, like he might gag.)* Oh good god — *(Josie smells it too. She puts her spring roll down.)*
JOSIE. Jesus!
ERIC. The wind shifted.
JOSIE. Shut it! *(Quickly, he does. He paces around the room, looking for the can of air freshener.)*
ERIC. See —
JOSIE. That smell …
ERIC. Barbecuing a computer.
JOSIE. What?
ERIC. That's how one of the firemen described it in the paper.
JOSIE. I don't think I could even describe that. Jesus …
ERIC. Not even an analogy?
JOSIE. *(Not joking.)* Not funny.
ERIC. Aha! *(He finds the can of air freshener behind one of the boxes and starts to spray like a maniac.)*
JOSIE. Eric —

ERIC. What?
JOSIE. The food?
ERIC. It's air freshener!
JOSIE. I don't want my spring roll tasting like a fresh country morning. *(He finishes spraying. There is a deadly lull as they look at their food. Neither of them go to eat it. Eric grabs 2 Diet Cokes out of the take-out bag and places them on the box. Josie smiles and takes the Diet Coke, as does Eric.)*
ERIC. So how's the hubby?
JOSIE. OK.
ERIC. Just OK. Not the usual ringing endorsement of married life.
JOSIE. I guess were sorta fighting now.
ERIC. *(Excited.)* Really? About what?
JOSIE. We went out for the first time last weekend. To a dinner party at Lisa's ... something she'd originally scheduled for the week of the 11th —
ERIC. How was that?
JOSIE. At first, it was great. Everyone was so excited to see everyone. None of us live or work anywhere downtown so it's not like any of us were in danger but everyone was being so ... grateful.
ERIC. On the Upper East Side even.
JOSIE. Lisa even got teary when we arrived.
ERIC. *(Fake moved.)* That is so touching ...
JOSIE. Eric — She was genuinely emotional about it. And not just her. Everyone was being so sincere and thoughtful and interested in everything you had to say. It was kinda freaking me out.
ERIC. I'm sure.
JOSIE. But once we had some drinks and settled into dinner it got a little more back to normal. That's when David and I got in a major fight.
ERIC. Over what?
JOSIE. He started telling my story.
ERIC. Again?!
JOSIE. I told him that it was sorta funny once but not over and over and especially not at someone else's dinner party. But he just thinks its hysterical that I went and got my hair done after the second plane hit. Fucking hysterical. It's not that ridiculous, right?
ERIC. I went to vote after the second plane.
JOSIE. See — People were going about their business. We all knew it was serious but I remember thinking, sure it's this enormous

23

fire, but they'll put it out. That's what the fire department does. They put out fires.
ERIC. And then I went to the deli. Got a bagel and a Diet Coke.
JOSIE. That's what I mean! We had no idea. No fucking idea. It didn't seem like some major national crisis. But David thinks it's the most hysterical fucking joke — the nation's under attack and Josie needs her roots touched up. Ba-dump.
ERIC. That's totally not fair.
JOSIE. Fucking right it's not. I mean I made that appointment two months ago. Do you know how hard it is to see Jean-Luc?
ERIC. Alright — that might not be helping your case.
JOSIE. Anyway, when we got home I just let that fucker have it. I told him that he had no right to tell that story again and make a fucking mockery of my goddamn hair appointment.
ERIC. Yikes — so what happened?
JOSIE. Basically, it killed our sex life.
ERIC. I thought everyone was copulating like bunnies — end of the world and all.
JOSIE. Frankly, we haven't been having sex at all since the 11th. The fight just gave us a more concrete reason for not having sex.
ERIC. Wow. So why did you stop?
JOSIE. I don't know … we talked about it a few days after the 11th and we … we didn't feel sexy. We just felt … I don't know. Alive. But kind of a sad alive. *(Josie looks at Eric, inviting him to join the conversation. He looks away, uncomfortably, and fishes for his cigarettes. He holds the pack up to Josie.)*
ERIC. Do you —
JOSIE. Maybe one. *(Complicit, she lights up as does Eric but smokes somewhat delicately, like a nonsmoker.)* Were you smoking at Will's?
ERIC. No way — he'd throw me out.
JOSIE. It was really nice of him to take you in like that.
ERIC. Take me in? He dragged me to Brooklyn. Against my will.
JOSIE. Because you were freaking out here.
ERIC. I was fine.
JOSIE. That's not what he told me.
ERIC. You guys talked?
JOSIE. He called me that night. He was really worried about you. Said you weren't making a lot of sense.
ERIC. I was tired. That's all.
JOSIE. Did you guys sleep together while you were there?

ERIC. No.
JOSIE. No?
ERIC. The first night I was sprawled on the couch watching TV and he said that I could sleep in his bed if I wanted.
JOSIE. So nothing happened.
ERIC. Nope. I just curled up next to him and he held me.
JOSIE. *(Thinking.)* Are you thinking about —
ERIC. No. No! We are not getting back together.
JOSIE. I don't know — maybe that would be a good thing right now.
ERIC. Josie — please don't say that.
JOSIE. Considering all you've been through.
ERIC. I'm fine.
JOSIE. You are now … probably because Will got you out of here. Can you imagine if you'd been here alone that whole week after when everything —
ERIC. Can we not get into this … please.
JOSIE. Look — you know I'm not Will's biggest fan but he took care of you. Let you stay at his apartment when you were freaking out about being here. He was actually a mensch.
ERIC. What?
JOSIE. A good guy. Maybe you need a good guy right now.
ERIC. Or a good roommate.
JOSIE. You think that Brit's gonna spoon with you and lullaby you to sleep?
ERIC. Let's not get crazy now … Will can't even sing.
JOSIE. Analogy.
ERIC. Uh, not really but —
JOSIE. Just think about it. I worry about you being down here alone.
ERIC. I won't be much longer. I have to get someone by the 30th. Work has been non-existent. I can't afford to carry a full month's rent.
JOSIE. How's the landlord?
ERIC. Persistent.
JOSIE. Oh — that's sweet, given the circumstances. Jesus!
ERIC. I'm sure I'll get someone. I've never had trouble before.
JOSIE. You have had some difficulty securing a boyfriend.
ERIC. OK — I'm gonna smoke the whole pack now.
JOSIE. Joking.
ERIC. *(Not really laughing.)* Oh — ha ha ha. *(Josie looks at him intensely.)*

JOSIE. Just think about it …
ERIC. What?
JOSIE. Will.
ERIC. No. Way.
JOSIE. Then eat. *(Blackout.)*

Scene 3

In the darkness, the answering machine is heard.

ANSWERING MACHINE. Tuesday, 10:05 A.M.
JEREMY. *(Voiceover.)* Hullo. Jeremy calling. I'm afraid I have some dreadful news. I've been laid off from my job at the St. Regis. There's been an utter lack of guests due to "recent events" so it looks like I'll be returning to London rather prematurely. But I do want to thank you for being so kind and showing me your splendid flat. Good luck with everything. Cheers. *(Lights up on the apartment. No one is in it.)*
ANSWERING MACHINE. Tuesday, 2:37 P.M.
KEVIN. *(Voiceover.)* What's up — it's Kevin again. Wanted to stop by and see the pad this afternoon if that's cool. Maybe bring the moving truck by around 5 or so and get myself settled by tonight. *(A beat.)* Naw — just kidding, just kidding. Anyway I'm gonna be downtown most of the day. So, like you said, I'll just stop by. Peace! *(Kevin enters the apartment and strides over to the window with Eric a few paces behind him. Kevin is a live-wire kind of guy, wearing a brown leather jacket with a concert T-shirt underneath. He is constantly moving and smoking a cigarette.)* Wow — this place is awesome!
ERIC. Really?
KEVIN. Shit yeah. It's great! Nice big space. Windows. Light.
ERIC. *(Staring at cigarette.)* You're a smoker then?
KEVIN. Oh. Yeah — is that a problem?
ERIC. Actually I'm trying to quit —
KEVIN. Shit, man. Me too. What's that line from *Airplane!* — Lloyd Bridges says?

ERIC. "I picked the wrong week to quit smoking"
KEVIN. Yeah, yeah, yeah — "I picked the wrong month to quit smoking." Ha ha ha … *(Kevin wanders over to the window. Some car honking is heard.)* So how's the noise?
ERIC. You know … New York. It's loud but you get used to it.
KEVIN. That's cool. I'm a New Yorker, man. I'm used to it.
ERIC. How long you been here?
KEVIN. About a year and a half.
ERIC. They say you need to be here at least two years to be a real New Yorker.
KEVIN. Not me. The minute I got here I was here, you know what I mean?
ERIC. *(Oooo-kay.)* Yeah … .so where are you living now?
KEVIN. Nowheres. Just going from couch to couch.
ERIC. You have a job then?
KEVIN. Shit yeah. What do you think I'm some kinda bum?
ERIC. No it's just that —
KEVIN. Just kidding. Just kidding. I gotta great job. I manage a trucking company over in Jersey City. It's my uncle's business and I've been running it for him since the beginning of the year. It's a great fucking job man. But these days, I just don't have a place to rest my weary ass. *(Kevin spies an ashtray filled with butts. He uses it to put his out.)* Quittin's going well …
ERIC. So you don't have an apartment now.
KEVIN. My place was down in Battery Park City.
ERIC. Oh —
KEVIN. Shouldn't say "was." It's still there, they just won't let us in yet. They told us that all the units are covered in dust. This layer of toxic crap on everything.
ERIC. Were you there when it happened?
KEVIN. No — thank god. I would have fucking freaked out! Not that I didn't freak out anyway. But I would have lost my shit if I was there. It's two blocks away, man. Fuck.
ERIC. So you'd already left for work?
KEVIN. Naww. I was in Jersey City. Had stayed there for a date Monday night. To meet this chick.
ERIC. *(Sorta shocked.)* Oh …
KEVIN. Uhhhm — you gay?
ERIC. Uh … yeah, but —
KEVIN. The ad didn't come out and say it but I can read between

the lines. Clean, quiet, responsible, seeks male ... Gay!
ERIC. *(Amused.)* Well ... gay as charged.
KEVIN. Gay as charged. That's a good one, man.
ERIC. Uh ... thanks. So ... you were having this date ...
KEVIN. Yeah — yeah — yeah — I'd met this girl Saturday night at a pool hall up on 19th. So we made plans to hookup at the Mall in Jersey City that Monday.
ERIC. How romantic.
KEVIN. I like going to the mall for dates. Grew up in the 'burbs so I'm kinda nostalgic for the mall scene. So we met at the Food Court and got some sandwiches at Arby's, strolled around and then headed back to her place in J.C.
ERIC. Sounds like a pretty successful first date.
KEVIN. Yeah — this chick was hot!
ERIC. Do you do that a lot?
KEVIN. Naww — I'm not into lots of one-night things usually. It's cool to have guests here, every now and then, right?
ERIC. Uh ... sure.
KEVIN. Oh cool. Cool. Cause I do like to have guests ... a few, you know, at least two every weekend. One Friday, one Saturday. *(A beat.)* Just kidding. Just kidding.
ERIC. *(Not.)* Funny. So you were at this "chick's" place when everything happened?
KEVIN. Yeah — we woke up and had sex a couple times. It was sooo hot, man. She had these amazing tits that were — *(Sees he's losing his audience.)* Anyway, so she gets out of bed and turns the TV on and they're saying that some plane hit the World Trade Center. I'm thinking, you know, like a prop plane or something.
ERIC. That's what everyone thought.
KEVIN. Right — and she's convinced it's like a bigger plane 'cause of all the smoke. But I'm like how could a serious-sized plane with commercial pilots make that kinda mistake. The sky was crystal clear — so my theory was that it was some drunk in a prop plane. And so we're arguing about it when bam. Right there on the TV, the other plane hits. Right there. Bam. Like an answer to our argument. Then I start freaking out about my apartment building. So we got some clothes on and went down to the waterfront and were there for, I don't know, ten minutes when we saw the first one come down. That was fucking insane! I'm standing there, looking at my apartment building as this huge

grey cloud just swallows it. The place disappeared. For a while there, I thought it was gone, you know … .just crushed or something. I was sorta losing it you know. Thinking … man, there goes everything. *(Kevin grows unexpectedly quiet and seems a little lost. Nervously, Eric tries to change the subject.)*
ERIC. *(Changing the subject.)* So whattya think of the place? Do you like it?
KEVIN. Sure. Long as we can get along. Let's see … .uh, are drugs a problem?
ERIC. What?
KEVIN. I smoke pot sometimes. Is that cool?
ERIC. *(Not really but …)* Well … uh, sure.
KEVIN. Cool. Cool. I mean sometimes, I'll do a little coke. Some crystal too. Maybe some speed — *(A beat.)* Just kidding. Just kidding.
ERIC. You're a real kidder, huh?
KEVIN. *(Seriously.)* Yeah. But seriously, the pot's cool, right?
ERIC. *(On balance …)* Umm … sure.
KEVIN. You can have some too if you want.
ERIC. *(Shaking his head.)* Makes me paranoid. Which I definitely don't need these days.
KEVIN. That's cool. Just wanted to be friendly. If I'm gonna have a roommate, I wanna be friends with them, you know, hanging out. You like to hang out?
ERIC. *(Fudging.)* Well … my schedule can be pretty busy sometimes.
KEVIN. Relax. I don't mean like every night, man.
ERIC. Oh. *(A relieved beat.)* Yeah. That would be … cool.
KEVIN. Cool. Cool. We'll get along then. *(An anxious, pacing beat.)* So … how'm I doing?
ERIC. Huh?
KEVIN. I think it's going good. We can get along, right?
ERIC. I guess I —
KEVIN. I like to get along with my roommates. It's a necessity in this city. And now, with all that's going on it's really important. I mean, we're at fucking war man. So when you come home, you know, you gotta be able to have some peace. I mean people are dead out there. Thousands of 'em. Right on my fucking doorstep. That's some intense shit. And I just need some goddamn peace in my life right now, you know what I mean? *(Kevin is looking at Eric, seeming a little crazed now. Eric looks away.)*

ERIC. So ... what happened with that girl in Jersey City?
KEVIN. Huh? Oh — her? Nothing.
ERIC. Nothing?
KEVIN. It was supposed to be a date, you know. A fling thing. Then I got stuck out there. The PATH was gone, the ferries out, tunnels closed. I couldn't get back into the city 'til Friday. So it became this endless three-day relationship. A fucking nightmare.
ERIC. But you spent the 11th with her ...
KEVIN. And the 12th, 13th and 14th. *(A beat.)* That was the problem, man. It was all too insane. I mean where can a relationship go from there?
ERIC. I was at my boyfriend's for that whole week.
KEVIN. Whoa — you gotta boyfriend?
ERIC. No. Did I say that?
KEVIN. It's cool ... that's cool.
ERIC. He's my "ex" boyfriend. I can't believe I said that.
KEVIN. You stayed at your ex's place?
ERIC. For a whole week.
KEVIN. Man — that sounds like a nightmare.
ERIC. He was insistent. Practically dragged me out of here.
KEVIN. So you were here when it happened?
ERIC. Oh yeah — saw the whole thing out that window.
KEVIN. Shit ... it must have been fucking crazy being this close.
ERIC. It was a scene down here. The neighborhood was like some kinda war zone; all these FBI and police vans and fire trucks and dump trucks. Parked in front of my building!
KEVIN. Yeah?
ERIC. *(Uncharacteristic outburst.)* Oh my god — that's when I started, you know, freaking out a bit. I mean ... seeing all that, in front of your house. These camouflage soldiers and tanks —
KEVIN. *(Semi-unnerved.)* Tanks?!
ERIC. *(More hysterical.)* I mean the National Guard was sitting on my stoop, with semi-automatic rifles! That were loaded. With live ammunition and — *(The phone rings interrupting this rant.)*
ERIC. Hello! Uh ... Warren? Hi ... yeah ... I'm showing it all this week. *(He checks his watch.)* Uh sure — that would be good. Great. See you then! *(Eric hangs up and turns to Eric.)*
ERIC. Sorry — I got another person coming over in ten minutes.
KEVIN. Boy you're just bringing 'em in and kicking 'em out. *(A beat.)* Jus' kiddin', jus' kiddin'. So, uh, I'll give you a call tomorrow?

ERIC. Uh ... sure.
KEVIN. Cool — I really dig the place. You seem cool.
ERIC. Uh ... thanks.
KEVIN. I think this could work. I hope so, man. It's two weeks and I still don't have anywhere to go. My back is fucking killing me from all these couches. I just wanna — I wanna go home, you know.
ERIC. I know what you mean.
KEVIN. But you've got a home. Your place is still here and you survived fuckin' intact.
ERIC. Looks that way, doesn't it? *(A beat.)* It just doesn't feel like the same place ... I probably shouldn't complain.
KEVIN. Yeah. You shouldn't.
ERIC. Hey — I'm really sorry about your apartment.
KEVIN. Yeah ... thanks, man. *(A beat.)* Fucking Osama. At least we're gonna kick his ass now, man.
ERIC. You think they'll actually get him?
KEVIN. If they do, I wanna be the first in line to fuckin' kick him in the balls. Well ... peace man.
ERIC. Yeah ... peace. *(Blackout.)*

Scene 4

In darkness, the answering machine is heard.

ANSWERING MACHINE. Wednesday, 10:52 A.M.
VICTOR. *(Voiceover.)* Hey — this is Victor. Thanks for showing me the place yesterday. I've been looking around all over the city at tons of places but I found somewhere that was a little more ... reasonable over in the East Village. Seems like there are some real bargains out there now. But good luck. I'm sure you'll find someone. It's a great location! Well ... take care and god bless.
ANSWERING MACHINE. Wednesday, 1:08 P.M.
KEVIN. *(Voiceover.)* Hey — what's up ... it's Kevin. Uh, just wanted to let you know I don't think I'll be moving in. That girl in Jersey City called and said I can stay with her for a bit. Can you fucking believe it? I mean, she's kinda insane but at least it's a bed

right? Anyway, thanks for showing me the joint. Peace. *(Lights up on the empty apartment. Eric is sitting on the floor, closing up some of the boxes. He is now wearing an unbuttoned long sleeve shirt over his t-shirt, something from J. Crew with stripes.)*

ANSWERING MACHINE. Wednesday, 2:31 P.M.

JEFF. *(Voiceover.)* Hey — Jeff Stone here, from Mark Green's campaign. We talked this morning. Anyway, I've gotta finish up some TV spots today. But I should be done around 3 or so ... maybe I can pop over then. Call me on my cell 646-321-8500 or you can send me an email to Jeff at green2001 dot org. That's 2-0-0-1-dot org. OK — see you later! *(The buzzer is heard and Eric gets it.)*

ERIC. Hey — come on up. The doors open! *(A moment later, Jeff enters the apartment, his outstretched hand leading the way. He is wearing a collared shirt and a tie and basic khakis with a work ID badge clipped to his belt.)*

JEFF. *(Shaking vigorously.)* Jeff Stone. Nice to meet you.

ERIC. Hi — Eric.

JEFF. So this is the room?

ERIC. Yep.

JEFF. I'll just take a look around.

ERIC. *(a look around?)* Okay ... *(Jeff starts to inspect the room like he works for the city or something. Checking up close to the floor and the walls, touching them, marking off the square footage, etc. Eric watches him somewhat bemused.)*

ERIC. So ... you're working for Mark Green.

JEFF. That's right.

ERIC. I voted for him. *(Jeff stops inspecting.)*

JEFF. Really? On the 11th?

ERIC. Yeah. After the second plane.

JEFF. That's ... um ... you're a serious voter.

ERIC. I'm a big believer in voting.

JEFF. Even during a crisis.

ERIC. Especially during a crisis. Once I'd figured out what was going on, that it was this terrorist thing, I got all determined and American about it — like, I'm not gonna let them try to stop me from voting.

JEFF. When I heard it was terrorists I thought they'd done it deliberately to disrupt the election.

ERIC. You know, I thought it was deliberate too. Part of the whole attack ... that's why I went to vote.

JEFF. I'm surprised you got to cast it. I heard most of the polling places downtown were chaos.

ERIC. It wasn't easy. The old ladies who flip through the registration books ... they couldn't even find my street. And they live here! They were pretending not to be bothered but you could tell, they were losing it just like everyone else.

JEFF. They must not have been losing it too much. They found your street ...

ERIC. Eventually. And I did cast my vote for democracy ... which in the end didn't even count.

JEFF. Just like the presidential race.

ERIC. Touché.

JEFF. Just make sure to vote next time. It'll count and we'll need it ... Bloomberg is getting a major bounce just because he's a Republican.

ERIC. Ugh — I can't stand Bloomberg. He seems kinda dippy, you know?

JEFF. Really — interesting. Why? *(Jeff gets out his Palm Pilot and takes a note.)*

ERIC. I don't know. He just does — hard to explain.

JEFF. *(Thinking out loud.)* Dippy ... good. We can use that.

ERIC. So what do you do for the campaign?

JEFF. I got sent up here to work on their media strategies team.

ERIC. From where?

JEFF. Oh — I was in Washington, working for the DNC. Got the call a couple weeks ago and here I am.

ERIC. They called in the cavalry, huh?

JEFF. Yeah — suddenly the campaign went from tough to impossible. It's hard now to say anything against the Republicans in general. Bin Laden's done more for the popularity of the Republican party than Ronald Reagan.

ERIC. And that's saying something. *(Jeff seems to be done walking around the perimeter of the room and inspecting it for imperfections. It passes.)*

JEFF. Well — the place looks great. What's the rent again?

ERIC. It's ... it's a thousand.

JEFF. What a steal ... 500 each!

ERIC. Sorry. It's a thousand each. It used to be 500 each a while ago. But then —

JEFF. Lemme guess ... Guiliani?

ERIC. Yep. Turned it around ... too much so.
JEFF. I have to say ... cleaning up the city is probably the one thing Guiliani did that was worthwhile. I grew up here and, back then, the place was a disaster.
ERIC. Where did you live?
JEFF. My parents had a loft on Broadway.
ERIC. Wow — is it still there?
JEFF. *(Shaking his head.)* Old Navy. But I can't complain. Soho's nice now. There's things to do. You should've seen this place in the 70s. It was desolate. On the weekends, we used to play football on Broadway, Spring was one end zone and Prince was the other. And there was no traffic. One time I was streaking down the sideline and Mike threw me this long bomb and I was about to score when I tripped over a homeless guy. New York sorta stopped at 14th Street back then and picked up south of Canal. In the 70s, everyone just fled ...
ERIC. I've been wondering if the 11th might be having the same effect.
JEFF. I don't think people are that freaked out.
ERIC. Usually, the first or second person I'd see would be writing a check on the spot. You're like the 10th and still ...
JEFF. Maybe everyone's feeling ... uncertain.
ERIC. I'm certain of one thing. I'm not gonna let this drive me outta the city. I mean where would I go, to one of the boroughs?
JEFF. Oh man — you don't wanna do that.
ERIC. I know — everyone's all like Astoria is affordable, Williamsburg is soooo cool. But if I wanted to live in the suburbs and commute into Manhattan, I'd move back in with my parents.
JEFF. I feel the same way. Manhattan or bust.
ERIC. Otherwise ... what's the point.
JEFF. What's the point ... exactly.
ERIC. I mean Brooklyn ... it's so damn quiet out there.
JEFF. You go out there a lot?
ERIC. Not anymore, thank god. My ex is there.
JEFF. Ah ...
ERIC. Do you have an ex ... or a current ... or ... whatever.
JEFF. Uh no. Not seeing anyone now. Too busy with the campaign.
ERIC. I mean, if you did that's fine. Girlfriends or boyfriends ... they're fine.
JEFF. Except yours.

ERIC. He's fine. Just not right now. *(There is an awkward moment here, post-boyfriend. Jeff looks at the window and walks over towards it.)*
JEFF. Have you been down there yet?
ERIC. No. Definitely not. *(A remembering beat.)* Last time I was down there was about a month before the 11th. A few weeks after the breakup I went with a friend of mine on a shopping spree.
JEFF. Century 21?
ERIC. Oh yeah. I think we were the only New Yorkers there … it was August and the city was empty. Except for French tourists. I got some underwear and socks super cheap. That made me feel a lot better. It was a crummy day out, rainy and humid, so then we wandered around the underground shopping mall, got some summer clearance stuff at J. Crew. I bought this shirt there … my last purchase. *(Touches the shirt, thinking.)* Later it cleared up and we got some Krispy Kremes and just sat on that big awful plaza eating donuts and checking out all the hot French guys. God — that was such a nice lame afternoon. Who woulda ever thought that shopping at a mall would be so … evocative.
JEFF. We had an event down there yesterday with Mark and some of the firefighters.
ERIC. God — that must have been creepy.
JEFF. The strangest thing though … there were tons of people down there. Not at the site but as close as they can get, at Broadway and Chambers Street.
ERIC. That is just so … bizarre.
JEFF. I don't know how effective our event was. Those people weren't there to meet Mark, even with the firemen around. They were just there … looking.
ERIC. What is there to see?
JEFF. Not much actually. For 220 stories there really isn't much left. From where I was standing, I could see a pile of rubble about 50 feet — *(Eric's mood changes abruptly and he turns away from Jeff.)*
JEFF. Sorry — did I …
ERIC. Can we not talk about this?
JEFF. Sure. Sorry. *(A beat.)* Here I am blabbin' on like an idiot about our dumb photo op …
ERIC. It's your job. I'm sure the campaign is all about getting good images. I'm a photographer myself.
JEFF. Professionally?
ERIC. Not for the media or anything. I mainly do headshots, stills

on movie sets, promotional stuff for TV shows.
JEFF. Wow — that sounds exciting.
ERIC. It used to be ... but now ... I don't know.
JEFF. I think everyone's having doubts about their day job lately.
ERIC. It's more than doubts. I mean, a couple days after everything, I seriously considered joining the Air Force.
JEFF. *(Laughing.)* Really?
ERIC. Why is that so funny?
JEFF. I don't know—it just seems like a big leap from still photography to the armed forces.
ERIC. I guess it was a crazy idea. But the fact that I even thought it. Me ... flying some jet plane around — *(A smiling beat.)* Alright ... it is pretty hysterical.
JEFF. After everything happened, all I wanted to do was get back here.
ERIC. Really — why?
JEFF. All I kept thinking that day was that I wanted to be in New York. I mean I know D.C. had — but this is home.
ERIC. Believe me — you should be glad you missed it.
JEFF. Maybe ... but having grown up here I felt like I had to get back as soon as possible. It was like there had been a death in the family. I mean I didn't know anyone who was killed. But that's exactly what it felt like. So when this job came up, I jumped at it. Even though I had nowhere to live here anymore ... my parents moved upstate years ago. But I just had to be here, you know ... back home.
ERIC. But don't you think being here now ... it's just so depressing.
JEFF. It can be. But still ... at least now I feel like I'm part of everything that's happening, for better or for worse. That's what I wanted — to be here, doing something constructive, keeping democracy rolling along. Geez — that sounds corny but ... that's what this is all about, isn't it? The fact that this is my job, helping people get elected — in New York even — must drive them crazy. So it's the least I can do, right? *(Jeff picks up his BlackBerry pager. There is a message.)*
JEFF. Sorry — gotta get back to the office. New polls came in.
ERIC. Oh ... is there anything else you wanted to know?
JEFF. Other than ways to reduce the rent —
ERIC. Uh, I don't think —
JEFF. Actually, I think this could work out. And I really need

something quick. Since I got here, I've just been sleeping at campaign headquarters.
ERIC. On what?
JEFF. The floor.
ERIC. Ouch!
JEFF. It's not so bad. There's a relatively new carpet and the desk is over my head. I pull a few filing cabinets over to block the light and it's almost cozy. Sorta like camping but not as much fun … Anyway, this is a great place and you seem like a relatively normal and sane guy.
ERIC. Relative to what?
JEFF. What's going on in the world of course.
ERIC. *(Nervously stumbling.)* Oh good — yeah I'm fine. I mean, I — I'm much better. I mean, I'm gonna be — *(Jeff is checking his pager again, tapping something into it and doesn't notice Eric's bit of nervousness here.)*
JEFF. So when do you need to know?
ERIC. Uh … as soon as possible?
JEFF. I'm swamped in the next few days … how 'bout we talk on Friday.
ERIC. *(Unsure.)* Uh … okay. I don't know if I can hold it …
JEFF. Well if it's still open, let's talk then … and don't forget to vote.
ERIC. As long as I'm here, I'll be voting.
JEFF. Where you going?
ERIC. Nowhere … gallows humor.
JEFF. Right — understandable these days.
ERIC. A necessity. (Blackout.)

Scene 5

In darkness, the answering machine is heard.

ANSWERING MACHINE. Wednesday, 9:46 P.M.
WILL. *(Voiceover.)* Hey — Will here. Just wanted to see how the roommate hunt is going. Maybe you should try Rainbow Roommates. Now I know it sounds kinda gay but a friend of mine

here at work used them and found a decent professional roommate in a couple days. Anyway ... give it a shot. And if it doesn't work out I can always move in. Okay — that was a joke. Alright, maybe half-joking. Call me!

ANSWERING MACHINE. Thursday, 3:12 P.M.

JOEY. *(Voiceover.)* Hi Joey again! From Rainbow Roommates?! Anywho, the place looked fabulous and I looooove that neighborhood. It's so neighborhood-y? But you won't believe this! Remember that audition for the road company of *Beauty and the Beast* I had — I got the part!? Ahhh — can you believe it?! Sorry I'm spazzing all over your little machine! I just found out and didn't want to leave you hanging. You were a super sweet guy, really, and I'm sure you'll find the most amazing roommate! Bye! *(Lights up inside the apartment. It is evening outside the window. Josie enters and crosses to the window. She is holding a small brown paper bag. As the answering machine plays, Josie reacts to the next crazy message.)*

ANSWERING MACHINE. Thursday, 6:28 P.M.

CARLOS. *(Voiceover.) Buenos dias* — it's your landlord calling for my formerly favorite tenant. What's going on with the rent, amigo? I need to get this squared away ... it's going on two weeks now. And the first is coming up. Roommate or no, I got bills to pay. And I need money ... real American money. Not Canadian. Not Español. What is that song goes ... *(Singing, landlord style.) Money makes the world go round, the world go round, the world go round. (A beat.)* Call me and let me know when I can expect that check. Goodbye.

JOSIE. It's still smoking ...

ERIC. *(Offstage.)* Yeah ...

JOSIE. It's like enough already. We get it, you know. But there it is ... still smoking. I mean, can't they stop it?

ERIC. *(Offstage.)* It stops. Then they remove stuff and oxygen gets in and it starts again. *(Eric enters the room.)*

JOSIE. You still smoking?

ERIC. If it's still smoking, I'm still smoking.

JOSIE. Ok — that was beyond tasteless.

ERIC. Sorry. My sense of humor is a little off these days.

JOSIE. Seriously ... I don't know how can you still live down here. *(Thinking.)* Maybe you should think about getting a place uptown. Near us!

ERIC. 82nd Street?! I get nosebleeds above 14th.
JOSIE. Sure but — you still haven't found a roommate. And what about the landlord?
ERIC. He's fine.
JOSIE. He didn't sound fine. Do you need me to lend you money?
ERIC. No — he's always getting on my case, jibing me like that. It's a power play thing, you know. Like he's in charge.
JOSIE. Eric — he is in charge.
ERIC. He's not gonna throw me out or anything. I'm his favorite tenant …
JOSIE. Former favorite …
ERIC. He was joking, okay?
JOSIE. If you need help —
ERIC. It's fine. I'm fine. *(Josie looks him over. Clearly, he's not looking so fine.)*
JOSIE. Did you call that 800 number yet?
ERIC. *(Sharp.)* Do you think I wouldn't have told you if I did?
JOSIE. Jesus … forget I asked.
ERIC. So what's in the bag? More food?
JOSIE. Sorta. You sounded a little desolate on the phone so I thought I'd cheer you up. *(Eric opens the bag. He smiles broadly.)*
ERIC. Cupcakes. From Magnolia?
JOSIE. Only the finest in refined sugar for you.
ERIC. You're so sweet.
JOSIE. Ba-dump. *(Eric takes one and starts eating. Heaven for minute. Then —)*
JOSIE. So — have you talked to Will?
ERIC. *(Eating.)* Mmmm … every day.
JOSIE. Wait a minute — you guys are talking every day now?
ERIC. On the phone. It's no big deal.
JOSIE. Who calls who?
ERIC. I don't know … .I guess he usually calls me.
JOSIE. That's good.
ERIC. Josie … we are not getting back together.
JOSIE. Did I say that?
ERIC. He's worried about me finding a roommate. That's all.
JOSIE. Still — his concern is sweet.
ERIC. He's just having ex-boyfriend guilt. I'm just having survivor's guilt. How bout you?
JOSIE. I'm having no-sex guilt.

ERIC. You had another fight with David?
JOSIE. Not exactly.
ERIC. So you discussed the sex-thing?
JOSIE. He did. At a party.
ERIC. Again?!
JOSIE. Yeah — Becky had some people over for cocktails last night. We were standing around in the kitchen having a civil conversation about some *New Yorker* article about how everyone's relationships right now seem to be either falling apart or coming together. And then my charming husband just offers up, you know, says right outta the blue — "Yeah, kinda like us not having had sex this month."
ERIC. Whoa.
JOSIE. He'd had a few drinks and —
ERIC. That's no excuse.
JOSIE. Beck's face just blanched.
ERIC. That is so out of bounds.
JOSIE. And then as I'm standing there, stunned, he kinda gave me this look of, aha — that got ya! Which is just so unnecessary.
ERIC. And totally wrong ... discussing that in front of your friends?
JOSIE. The stupid thing is that he just won't come out and say it.
ERIC. Well ... it sounds like that's exactly what he did.
JOSIE. No. The sex is more of a symptom.
ERIC. What's the problem then?
JOSIE. Kids.
ERIC. But I thought you'd decided ...
JOSIE. That we'd wait. 'Til he gets promoted, til we can get a house, 'til we're both a little older so we don't fuck up our kids the way our parents fucked us up.
ERIC. And now he's changed his mind ... post-everything?
JOSIE. Yep. Suddenly his clock is ticking.
ERIC. Everyone's clock is ticking ...
JOSIE. Except mine. If anything, I'm more ambivalent about doing this now ... especially now.
ERIC. Really?
JOSIE. OK, first off I don't wanna have some tacky, patriotic 9/11 baby along with the rest of the city. The maternity wards are going to be packed come June. And they'll probably be giving out flags instead of cigars. I mean I love my country but this flag stuff everywhere. It's like living in Texas. I mean really — is this any world to bring a child into?

ERIC. No. But remember our fucked up parents?
JOSIE. How can we forget …
ERIC. It was 1968 when we were born; Robert Kennedy, Martin Luther King, all the riots, the Chicago Convention, Vietnam … and Richard Nixon won! It was an insane time.
JOSIE. Maybe they were totally high or something and didn't even think about what the fuck they were doing.
ERIC. Your parents … maybe. Mine were in Delaware. Not much weed being passed around the PTA meetings.
JOSIE. They had weed in Delaware!
ERIC. Irrelevant. So the bottom line here is you don't wanna get pregnant right now?
JOSIE. *(Hesitating.)* More or less.
ERIC. More or less … whaddya —
JOSIE. Wait a minute — don't tell me that you, of all people, are going to try and convince me that I should have a child?
ERIC. Why not — I mean you said you wanted to have kids eventually. Maybe this is eventually.
JOSIE. This is now. Eventually is … eventually.
ERIC. Josie —
JOSIE. *(Like a parlor game.)* Give me one good reason why I should have a kid now. Go! Go!
ERIC. Uh … uhmmm … Jesus Josie … okay … *(An "aha" beat.)* Okay — you know how I'm always saying that I wanna be a fake uncle, like people calling me "Uncle Eric" when I'm not related at all and then the kid being totally confused and wondering, when he gets older, why he thought this strange gay guy was his uncle when clearly there's no blood relation whatsoever and the only reason he was being called "Uncle" was because his mom thought it was cute to have her best friend be quasi-related to her baby?
JOSIE. Ranting …
ERIC. That's a pretty good ranty-reason.
JOSIE. It's pretty Hallmark when you boil it down a bit.
ERIC. I was trying to disguise it … thus the rant.
JOSIE. *(To herself almost.)* Your rants are always meant to disguise something.
ERIC. What do you mean?
JOSIE. C'mon Eric … whenever you're getting all emotional about something you try to cover it up with some crazily-worded rant.

ERIC. I do?
JOSIE. Ohmygod — especially in the last month. You have been rant central. That's why I'm worried about you.
ERIC. But I'm fine ...
JOSIE. You say that. But I always have this sense that ... I don't know. You're hiding something.
ERIC. *(Heavy sigh.)* Great.
JOSIE. What? So you are?
ERIC. That's exactly what Will said.
JOSIE. Eric ... I didn't talk to Will about this. I haven't talked to him since the night of the 11th. But honestly, that's what I've been worried about. That you've gone through all this crap — all of this incredibly sad stuff. And you don't seem sad. Just, I don't know, a little further away ...
ERIC. I am sad. I mean everyone's sad, right? It's like a given right now. *(Eric turns away from her, back to the window and concentrates on his cupcake. Josie, seeming a little unnerved by the strangely lived in look of the room. She notices some of his things on the floor; the cordless phone, a book, about six deli cups of coffee, a full ashtray.)*
JOSIE. How much sleep did you get last night?
ERIC. Mmmmmmm ... these cupcakes are amazing.
JOSIE. Eric — when did you get up today?
ERIC. *(Indicating bag.)* Can I have yours?
JOSIE. No and answer my goddamn question.
ERIC. I don't know ... early.
JOSIE. And when did you go to sleep?
ERIC. I don't know ... late?
JOSIE. You stayed up again, pulling an anxiety all-nighter. Smoking and drinking coffee and watching the news.
ERIC. I still don't get any channels.
JOSIE. God — that's even worse ... just sitting around by yourself.
ERIC. I listened to NPR.
JOSIE. Public radio doesn't make it any better.
ERIC. It was only last night, really.
JOSIE. What happened last night?
ERIC. I ... I heard some sirens.
JOSIE. We live in Manhattan. There are always sirens.
ERIC. But now —
JOSIE. Nothing is gonna happen, Eric. The worst is over.
ERIC. We're at war Josie.

JOSIE. With who? The Taliban?! They don't even have an army ... they have camels. And those probably don't even work.
ERIC. They don't need an army. They're here. In sleeper cells. Waiting for a signal to kill more people. Just yesterday a guy in Florida died of anthrax. Anthrax! What about that?
JOSIE. Anthrax?! What the hell does that have to do with anything?! It was in the fucking everglades or something. In the middle of nowhere. What — you think there's gonna be some sort of anthrax attack here? *(Nervous "yes" silence.)* Okay — now you're not only being paranoid but you're missing the point. The point of terrorism is —
ERIC. Let the tutorial begin ... the point of terrorism is to —
JOSIE. Is to inflict terror. The only weapon they had was surprise. And they got their one great shot to do it. What was it Dan Rather said, they lost the war the minute that second plane hit. That was it. Game over.
ERIC. Thank you professor. But when I'm in bed, trying to sleep and I hear a bunch of sirens wailing I tend to think the worst. It's how the whole thing began for me. Hearing all those sirens, a thousand sirens going off. It was infinite sirens to the nth degree.
JOSIE. But can't you tell when it's just one siren, not a thousand.
ERIC. It's never one siren.
JOSIE. Alright — there's still a difference between three sirens and 3,000 sirens.
ERIC. Not at three-thirty in the morning! *(Josie gives up arguing this point. She turns and looks at the dresser.)*
JOSIE. You know what the problem is?
ERIC. Uh — you won't let me have your cupcake?
JOSIE. You've gotta get this stuff outta here. Wasn't Will gonna take the dresser?
ERIC. Maybe. He thinks it's ugly.
JOSIE. Once you get this old stuff out and get a new roommate, I'm sure you'll feel a lot better. Instantly.
ERIC. The trick now is actually getting the new roommate.
JOSIE. There's no trick. And now that things are getting back to normal and —
ERIC. Face it Josie. Things are not getting back to normal — they can't.
JOSIE. That's bullshit. People are going on with their lives ...
ERIC. Maybe above 14th Street.

JOSIE. And don't give me your whole Downtown DMZ rant ... you act like 14th Street is the friggin' Berlin Wall.
ERIC. *(Hysterical.)* Oh please — people up there have no idea. None!
JOSIE. Okay — you're getting hysterical again.
ERIC. Look — have you seen things getting back to normal down here? Have you?
JOSIE. Of course.
ERIC. Of course?! Are you kidding? Have you noticed the "Missing" flyers everywhere. Or the candles in front of every fire station. Or maybe the heavily armed storm troopers on every corner. *(Challenging.)* Give me one back-to-normal example. Go! GO!
JOSIE. Okay — let's see. Uh ... yesterday, I was coming out of the Mercer Hotel when this supermodel stole my cab, right out from under me.
ERIC. What did you do?
JOSIE. I called her a fashionista cunt.
ERIC. But did she call you anything back?
JOSIE. Jesus!
ERIC. *(I win!)* Aha! *(The phone rings, interrupting their argument. Josie checks her watch.)*
JOSIE. Who the hell is that at eleven-thirty at night?
ERIC. I don't know. Let's take a look. *(Eric picks up the phone and looks at the caller ID.)*
JOSIE. Is it Will?
ERIC. Definitely not. *(Josie looks at the Caller ID on Eric's prompting.)*
JOSIE. What the hell is the "Triple X Pony"?
ERIC. A video book store on West Street.
JOSIE. A porn store!?
ERIC. A full service gay porn store.
JOSIE. They still have those? *(Eric picks up the phone and answers.)*
ERIC. Hello — yes — yes — oh hi, Alex. Yeah — I remember. Right. Uh-huh. Tonight? Yeah. It's in Soho. Uh — okay. Twelve, sounds good. See you then.
JOSIE. Who the hell is Alex?
ERIC. *(Nonchalant.)* Guy coming to see the apartment.
JOSIE. *(Imitating.)* Oh ... "guy coming to see the apartment." *(A beat.)* Try freaky porn-fiend coming over to rape you.
ERIC. Josie! I talked to him earlier today. He wants to see the place.
JOSIE. At midnight?!

ERIC. It's not like I can afford to turn anyone away. I have to decide by tomorrow.
JOSIE. You know what, sometimes caller ID is more than anyone needs to know. *(Eric springs into action, handing Josie the cupcake bag and starting to hustle her towards the door.)*
ERIC. Well ... thanks for the cupcakes and "cheer."
JOSIE. Wait — I'm leaving?
ERIC. He's gonna be here in 10 minutes. I gotta clean up.
JOSIE. But can't I meet him?
ERIC. Josie —
JOSIE. I can help you decide.
ERIC. Lately the only thing that helps them decide is the rent.
JOSIE. Alright. But don't let him bargain you down?
ERIC. Even if he offers me his body?
JOSIE. Maybe I should stay.
ERIC. Goodnight Josie. *(He turns her towards the door.)*
JOSIE. Why can't I stay?
ERIC. Because you don't live here.
JOSIE. Call me tomorrow. I wanna know everything.
ERIC. Josie — it's not a date. It's a potential roommate.
JOSIE. Let's hope so.
ERIC. Goodnight. And get home safe.
JOSIE. *(Stopping.)* Alright — you never used to say that before.
ERIC. And don't take the subway! *(Blackout.)*

Scene 6

In darkness, we hear the answering machine.

ANSWERING MACHINE. Friday 12:32 A.M.
ALEX. *(Voiceover.)* Hi — Alex down here on the corner. Oh — I hope it's not too late to see the apartment. I think I'm lost but — oh wait that's it right here. I thought I was — okay never mind. I'll see you in a sec. *(The buzzer goes off and the lights go up. Eric is sitting on the floor reading a magazine and drinking a big traveler mug of coffee. He gets up and hits the intercom.)*

ERIC. Yeah?
ALEX. *(Offstage.)* It's Alex.
ERIC. Okay — come on in. Third floor. *(Eric hits the buzzer. Using the window as a mirror he takes a look at his appearance; he is dressed in jeans and the J. Crew shirt over his t-shirt. He seems dissatisfied with this look. He fixes his hair, unbuttons a few buttons and looks in the window again. Still not good. He takes the shirt off. Looks in the window — good. He then rushes offstage again to unlock the door, which we can hear. He comes back into the room and starts to move things around, to make it look like he's been working in the room. A knock is heard.)*
ERIC. 'S open!
ALEX. *(Offstage.)* Hello?
ERIC. Back here …
ALEX. *(Offstage.)* Hellooo?
ERIC. Back. Here. *(Alex enters the room somewhat tentatively. He is young, eager and a very sharply put-together corporate kind of guy wearing a fitted suit with a colorful tie. He is not a freaky porn fiend at all. He notices Eric cleaning up.)*
ALEX. Hey —
ERIC. Hi — just trying to clean up in here a little.
ALEX. Is this a bad time to —
ERIC. Oh no. No. It's fine. You're fine. *(He didn't just say that.)* I mean … come on in. *(They check each other out. There is some real chemistry here between them. It makes for an awkward moment of silence which they both try to fill. The next line is said simultaneously.)*

ERIC.	ALEX.
So —	So —

ALEX. Sorry I'm so late.
ERIC. S'ok. I'm a bit of a night owl lately. *(Trying to ask innocently.)* So…what's keepin' you up tonight?
ALEX. Oh … uh … just working late. So … this is the room then?
ERIC. Yep — uh, let's see. There's a cable hook up there. And a phone jack in the corner. The A/C works if you want that too. I took it out so I could shut the window … the smell was —
ALEX. And how much is it?
ERIC. The A/C. It's free. The unit's been here for —
ALEX. No. How much is the rent?
ERIC. Oh. Uh … it's — it's about 1100?
ALEX. About?

ERIC. Plus utilities. 20 in the winter. 40 or so in the summer. *(An anxious beat.)* So ... would that work for you?
ALEX. Oh yeah. Definitely.
ERIC. Great. So ... where do you work?
ALEX. I'm at Goldman Sachs ... in the international bond division.
ERIC. Wow — sounds intriguing? *(À la 007 movies.)* Bond. International Bond.
ALEX. No ... just boring numbers crunching stuff. But it pays well.
ERIC. Thus the suit ...
ALEX. This? I got it at Century 21.
ERIC. That place is great. Was great. But I heard it pretty much survived which is amazing being just across the street. I used to go there all the time ... and the mall too. Got this shirt there, at the J. Crew store. God — it must be a mess down there, what's left of it. I can't even imag — *(Alex does not want to talk about this stuff and heads towards the window.)*
ALEX. Nice view ...
ERIC. Oh. Yeah ... it is pretty nice. Used to be ... *(A beat.)* My old roommate said that I should put "WTC View" in the ad. He had just moved here from Ohio and couldn't believe the view. I thought that was cute because, you know, no one ever puts that in apartment ads. You see Empire State view all the time ... it has some major value. But WTC View doesn't mean a thing. Didn't mean a ... but he kept saying that I should put it in. He thought it'd be this big selling point. WTC View ... *(Eric laughs a bit at this. Alex's mood shifts immediately, going somber, as he steps back from the window.)*
ALEX. It's not something to joke about.
ERIC. Oh ... I, uh ... .sorry. *(Alex notices all the boxes and stuff on the floor.)*
ALEX. So what's the deal with this stuff?
ERIC. My ex-boyfriend is gonna take the dresser.
ALEX. Oh — I'm sorry.
ERIC. You actually want the dresser?!
ALEX. No — about the ex. When did you break up?
ERIC. A couple months ago.
ALEX. *(Almost proud.)* I just broke up with my boyfriend too.
ERIC. Oh ... really. When did you guys break up?
ALEX. A couple weeks ago.
ERIC. At least you can blame it on Bin Laden. *(Eric smiles on saying this, trying to be breezy. But Alex has a stony faced reaction.)*

ALEX. That's really not funny.
ERIC. I'm sorry I — I just meant to say that all of this, everything that's happening — it's really affected people's relationships you know. It's making people do some pretty strange things. I mean my best friend isn't sleeping with her husband, people are having three-night one night stands, ex-boyfriends are sleeping together and — *(Alex starts smiling.)* What?
ALEX. I can't believe we're talking about this sorta stuff.
ERIC. Well ... we could talk about the Yankees? They're doing great and are a huge distraction for everybody.
ALEX. *(Giving up.)* Alright. You see ... my ex, Larry, wanted us to move in together after the 11th. But I didn't. So ... that was it and we broke up.
ERIC. Funny. That's why me and Will broke up too. The moving-in issue. Not the 11th ... *(Anyway.)* So what was the problem with moving in for you?
ALEX. Larry and I had been going out for only a year and a half. I thought moving in at that point was way too soon.
ERIC. Me too. Maybe after two years ... maybe.
ALEX. Right? And then, with everything that's happened recently, my life has totally changed. My priorities are different. Everything is so upside down, you know?
ERIC. Oh I know ...
ALEX. And I can't ignore that and just pretend to go on like nothing happened.
ERIC. Having trouble getting "back to normal"?
ALEX. Exactly. *(They smile at each other, a sense of understanding. And maybe a sense of something more. Then, some sirens are heard and Eric heads towards the window.)*
ERIC. Uh-oh ...
ALEX. What?
ERIC. Does that sound like a lot of sirens?
ALEX. Uh — I don't know ... *(Eric heads over to the clock radio and turns it on.)*
ALEX. What are you doing?
ERIC. Just wanna see what's going on. *(Eric finds a music station, not a news station, playing a song like Britney Spears' "Oops I Did It Again."* Eric seems relieved and Alex looks at him puzzled.)*

---

* See Special Note on Songs and Recordings on copyright page.

ALEX. How 'bout 1010 WINS?

ERIC. In an emergency, I always go for a pop station. If it's something really serious, they'll interrupt programming like on the 11th. If not — [Britney]. *(An uneasy beat.)* Still — sounds like a lot of sirens. *(Eric goes back over to the window and looks out.)*

ALEX. When I first moved here, I'd call home and my parents were always like "turn off the TV while we're on the phone" and I was like ... .that's not the TV, Mom, it's the East Village.

ERIC. Life here has always been pretty loud. But lately, it's insane. Have you heard the planes?

ALEX. Huh?

ERIC. The F-15s. They've got them on a constant patrol over the city. I heard them Sunday around 4 in the morning ... shook my bed the sound was so loud. *(He turns towards the window.)* And I don't understand why they're flying over Ground Zero ... I mean, I think they're a little late you know. *(Eric laughs at bit at his joke and, turning around, looks at Alex and notices that same blank, nervous expression from before. Eric is mortified.)*

ERIC. I did it again.

ALEX. You really like talking about it, huh?

ERIC. My friends think I talk about it too much.

ALEX. I mean you've gotta move on at some point.

ERIC. But until I reach that point ... I think I have to talk about it. Read every article about it. Know every detail about it.

ALEX. I don't wanna know anything else. I saw enough on the 11th.

ERIC. We all did.

ALEX. But for me it was ... it's kinda freaky.

ERIC. So ... where were you?

ALEX. I was there.

ERIC. There? You mean, right there?

ALEX. I was in Tower One. *(Eric is speechless, mouth open, dumbfounded.)*

ERIC. But ... you ... you got out.

ALEX. *(duh.)* Well, yeah.

ERIC. Oh my god. So what — what happened? How did —

ALEX. I had no idea what was going on.

ERIC. But you were there ... in the tower ... what floor?

ALEX. Ninety-one.

ERIC. How's that possible? I mean, you were right there.

ALEX. I had an early meeting that morning to go over some new

49

bonds. The meeting ended around quarter of nine and —
ERIC. That's right when the — how did you get out?
ALEX. I was in the sky lobby and everyone was getting off the elevators, going to work. So I got in an empty elevator by myself and hit the Lobby button. And I'm just standing there, whistling and looking at my feet ... you know, elevator stuff. Then suddenly the whole thing comes to a stop and there's this huge whoosh of air then a low rumbling sound. And the lights and everything flicker off for a minute but then come back on. I tried to open the doors but they were stuck. And then I heard some voices coming from the speaker but it was all jumbled. Then there was another rumbling sound, not as big. After that I was beginning to think this is probably pretty serious but still I didn't know what was going on. A voice comes on the speaker that I can finally understand and says there's a fire and that someone's coming to get me. So I just stand there waiting. So I wait and wait and wait. No one comes. All I can see is this sliver of dusty light through the doors and I think, maybe I should try to open them again. So I did and they opened. Just like that. I couldn't believe it but all that time I was in the lobby. On the ground floor. So I walk out and look around and all the windows are smashed and there's all this smoke but there are no people. I mean no one is around. So I walk out to the plaza and there is just — all this ... luggage. Suitcases that are open and garment bags and business clothes and shoes ... so many pairs of shoes. Then I hear this huge thump behind me — almost like a mini-explosion. And about twenty feet away is what I guess is a body ... not cause it looks like one. But because of all the blood. So I look up and see two more coming down, holding up table cloths as these makeshift parachutes that would work for a few seconds and then ... don't. At that point I knew I should run but with all this carnage and things falling I didn't know where to go. I froze. Then, outta nowhere, I feel something on my wrist — something that's burning hot. I think I'm on fire for a minute, that some piece of something's hit me, but I turn around and there's this huge fireman grabbing me by the wrist and he starts running, dragging me behind him. I tried to slow down and turn around and see exactly what the hell's going on but the fireman yells "don't turn around!" And hearing that ... I just get shivers all over my body. So we're just booking — down Vesey, over to West Street. Even though we're running I feel cold all of a sudden. The

only part of my body that feels warm is my wrist where he's holding me, and it's really starting to hurt. Finally, we get to the river where all these fire boats are parked and I hear this enormous crack, like a clap of thunder. I turn around to see it falling — coming down into this insane cloud that starts barreling towards us. The fireman just about throws me on a fireboat but the cloud stops before it gets to us. So I'm sitting on the boat and just shaking … I'm so cold. And a nurse comes up to me, staring at me, and asks if I'm hurt and I look at my pants and there's all this blood but it's not mine — it's from the plaza. So she checks me out and I'm not hurt at all. Not a scratch. The only thing I had was this big bruise on my wrist from the fireman. From his grip. That's all.
ERIC. That's … that's just …
ALEX. Now you've got me talking too much about it.
ERIC. No — it's fine really. I mean, it's not fine. But … you lived. You're like the new definition of lucky.
ALEX. Yeah.
ERIC. I mean … you should be dead.
ALEX. But I'm not.
ERIC. But to be right there and see all that … it must've been horrible.
ALEX. *(A pensive beat.)* In a weird way, I think I'm lucky to have even gone through the whole thing because as awful as it all was, it's also been the most … incredible thing too.
ERIC. It … it has?
ALEX. Everything is different now. Everything. I mean — the whole thing has turned me totally inside out. It's like Dorothy, you know — I went from black and white to Technicolor in one day.
ERIC. Yeah?
ALEX. Oh yeah … life is suddenly more … vivid. And I notice things I never noticed before. Like every time I take the subway it's … so cool. I get on the train now and it's like — there is so much life in one car. People flirting with each other and reading great books for the first time and totally asleep cause they've been working a 12-hour shift. It's just the whole city in miniature. And, on top of the people, there's all these bizarre little things going on too. Did you know the 2 train makes this noise like the opening strains of "Somewhere" from *West Side Story*?
ERIC. Really?
ALEX. Yeah. Right as it's pulling out of the station, as the engine

starts up and it makes the notes of the song. *(Singing.) There's ... a ... place ...*
ERIC. You're kidding?
ALEX. Totally serious. It's a trip! I love taking the subway ... and I go all over town now. I used to just go to work and then go home. But now ... do you have any idea the number of things you can do in this city? Every night is an adventure. I don't know where I'll end up. And it's pushed me to do things I never thought I'd do before. Ever. I mean, I got rid of my boyfriend, my mortgage, my apartment, even my cell phone ... and I don't miss any of it! *(Eric stares at him.)* Oh god — you must think I'm crazy. But you know what? I don't care. I don't care anymore. It probably sounds strange but, despite everything that's happened, the world is a pretty incredible place these days. And now I'm just trying to figure out, you know, why I'm still here. There's got to be some reason why I'm here. I don't know what it is but I'm trying to find out ... every amazing day.
ERIC. Maybe this is it.
ALEX. Oh ... like this here. To rent the room. Who knows ... maybe you're right. *(Alex smiles warmly at Eric. Again, more flirting. Then, Alex wanders over to the boxes and looks at them.)* So your ex still hasn't gotten his stuff?
ERIC. No. It's my roommate's stuff.
ALEX. He must've left in a hurry.
ERIC. Actually, he was gonna move out on the 15th but he —
ALEX. Wait — I thought you said he's gone.
ERIC. *(Caught.)* Yeah. He's gone. *(A beat.)* He's really ... just ... gone. *(Eric looks towards the window. Then it hits Alex. Gone. Dead.)*
ALEX. You mean he —
ERIC. Well ... yeah. *(Alex sits down on hearing this.)*
ALEX. Oh my god. I'm so sorry. I —
ERIC. He was all ready to move out. On the 15th. Most of his stuff was packed up and ready to go. And then ...
ALEX. So ... where was he?
ERIC. Tower 1. A little higher up though.
ALEX. Oh man. I'm so sorry, Eric. *(A beat.)* You don't have to talk about it if you ...
ERIC. No. It's okay. I haven't been really talking about him lately and everyone's kinda scared to even bring it up around me anymore, all my friends that is, because I ... I sorta lost it for a while and

couldn't really deal with the whole thing ... it was all a little overwhelming. I mean by the end of that day I was just ... a wreck. Everything just kept going from bad to worse, exponentially, you know — first it was just a fire, then this explosion. Then when that first one fell ... that was like — I mean who would have thought that could happen? People were standing outside my window. Screaming. Like a horror movie. And I kept thinking it can't get worse ... Stephen's in Tower 1 and maybe he's hurt but he'll be okay. I mean one tower going ... that's gotta be as bad as it can get. And then ...
ALEX. God — that's just awful. Were you good friends with this guy?
ERIC. No ... not really. Just roommates. He was only here for a few months. He was doing temp work down there, at some financial firm. Temping ... can you believe it? Can you imagine being stuck at some job you don't even want to do and then ...
ALEX. So he was planning on moving out already?
ERIC. Living here was supposed to be temporary. A friend of his, this girl he knew from college, was moving to the city. They were in this punky band together, The Haggard. He said they were sorta B-52's-ish. He kept telling me that he was the Fred and she was the Kate. Anyway, she was coming and they needed a place to live as well as rehearse and so he found this enormous loft for them out in Bushwick. A huge cheap place in an old factory. I told him he was crazy to go all the way out there ... I mean, Brooklyn, right? But he was so excited about it. Excited to start rehearsing again with the band. They already had their first gig at some dive in Williamsburg ... on the twenty-second. *(Eric is getting visibly upset by relating this. This is making Alex visibly uncomfortable.)*
ALEX. Hey — are you ...
ERIC. It's so stupid that I should be so ... I hardly knew him. When he was living here, we barely saw each other we were on such different schedules. Will saw him maybe once before we broke up. Everyone joked that he was my imaginary roommate, that I'd made him up. But he was a great roommate ... was always cleaning stuff around the apartment, stuff I never realized was even dirty. I'd come home and voila — things would be sparkling clean and everything would smell like lemons. He was just so ... nice. *(A beat.)* I think it's true that dumb saying or song or whatever it was. It seems only the nice people die in things like this leaving all of us to hate ourselves for not being so nice.

ALEX. Hey c'mon ... you seem like a nice guy.
ERIC. Oh right — you barely know me.
ALEX. Still ... you don't seem like some terrible person.
ERIC. Gee thanks.
ALEX. That's not what I — you seem nice. That's all I'm saying. *(Turned away from Alex, Eric looks lost in his own mournful world. Not exactly crying but just ... lost.)*
ALEX. Why don't I get going and I'll —
ERIC. Actually, can you ... stay for a bit?
ALEX. Well uh —
ERIC. If you don't want to that's fine.
ALEX. It's just late and I — *(As Eric speaks, he starts to lose control of his emotions.)*
ERIC. Never mind I just ... lately I'm feeling so down ... and you are ... you just seem to have this ... this positive thing going on which is great ... and I feel so not positive lately ... all that happened just sorta weighs on me ... makes me feel ... I don't know ... almost paralyzed by everything ... so much so that sometimes I can't even walk ... sometimes I just feel so low that ... that I start to think ... I think that ... *(A beat.)* Do you really think I'm a nice guy? *(Alex nods. This only causes Eric to break down and start crying. Alex moves closer to him. Eric starts to cry even more. Alex touches his shoulder and then holds him. Eric starts sobbing loudly, his head on Alex's shoulder. Alex is holding him when Eric's legs start to buckle. Supporting his weight, Alex guides him to the floor as Eric continues to heave with sorrow. Music like the instrumental intro to the second verse of "Poses" by Rufus Wainwright can be heard very low.* Then, Alex lifts up Eric's head and looks at him. They are both very still, staring at each other. Slowly, the lights begin to fade. Once the stage has gone to black, the song continues to play for a minute or two in total darkness.)*

---

* See Special Note on Songs and Recordings on copyright page.

Scene 7

Dim lights come up. It is the dead of night, around 2:30 A.M. There are some business clothes scattered on the floor. Eric, wearing no shirt and a pair of boxer briefs, is sitting on a couple boxes stacked up at the window, staring out. After a few moments, Alex enters the room wearing a pair of boxers and a white tanktop-style undershirt. Looking for Eric, he spots him sitting on the boxes. Eric, engrossed in thought, is totally unaware of his presence. Alex speaks up.

ALEX. Hey ... *(Eric is startled by this and jumps a bit. He turns and sees that it's Alex.)* Sorry I —
ERIC. No, it's my —
ALEX. What's up?
ERIC. Couldn't sleep.
ALEX. Sorry — I tend to sprawl out a bit in bed.
ERIC. No — you were fine. It's just ...
ALEX. What?
ERIC. Everything. *(Alex pulls up a box next to him, curls up to him sleepily.)* You don't have to.
ALEX. No really ... it's okay. What's up?
ERIC. I ... I haven't slept with anyone since Will and I broke up.
ALEX. Ahhh ... so I'm the first.
ERIC. Yeah ... "the first". Ha. I thought when I broke up with Will I was gonna go crazy, you know, sleeping with all these hot guys or something. A freedom field day. But nothing happened.
ALEX. Nothing?
ERIC. It's like suddenly no one was even looking at me ... like I had the gay scarlet letter or "Broken-Up" on my chest.
ALEX. I dunno. Maybe that's not really what you wanted?
ERIC. Oh I wanted it alright — that's why I broke up with Will because I was feeling too ... constrained and trapped and scared that, you know, that this was IT! That I was an adult, in a relationship that had lasted for more than a few months ... was approaching 2 years. And that I was 33 years old. I thought that by now everything

would be settled and perfect and cozy. But it turned out to be the opposite. My birthday was in May and that's when Will and I started fighting and then I had trouble getting steady work and my old roommate moved out because he couldn't afford the rent anymore and then Stephen moved in which actually was great until … *(Indicating window.)* It's like I've been thrown back ten years into all that uncertainty and confusion of my twenties … like I'm living a bad board game. Go back five spaces and lose your mind. That's what I need … a "get-out-of-insanity free" card. *(Alex regards him a little warily.)*
ALEX. Maybe we should get back to bed …
ERIC. No … I won't be able to sleep.
ALEX. What … nightmares?
ERIC. *(Laughing.)* Hardly. People keep asking, are you having nightmares, are you having nightmares? But when I sleep it's just this great empty blackness. When life is this … this sorta day-mare, sleep is a blessing, a total holiday from reality.
ALEX. So why can't you sleep then?
ERIC. Oh, I can sleep … the trick is getting to sleep. I just lie there in bed and close my eyes and all I can see is the 11th … everything I saw happening over and over again in a loop. Especially that explosion. And then I'll hear a siren and I'll have to wait to hear if there're more. And then a truck will backfire and I'll be turning the news on. And the next thing you know, it's sunrise and the traffic picks up and it's too noisy to sleep anyway so I just give up.
ALEX. Not sleeping can really screw with your head. Maybe that's why you had that outburst before.
ERIC. *(Dismissive.)* Oh that — I have one of those every day. It's usually when no one's around, that's all. You just happened to be in the right place at the right time.
ALEX. It's not that funny, you know. I mean, you were seriously losing it there … I didn't think you were gonna stop crying. *(A gentle beat.)* Maybe you should get some help. They have this 800 number.
ERIC. *(Wearily.)* Oh, I've heard about the number.
ALEX. I mean it's been a big help for me.
ERIC. I'm sure it's great for you and other victims and people who really knew people who died.
ALEX. Like your roommate … *(This stops Eric cold, as if he'd for-*

gotten this fact and was just reminded of it. Alex looks at Eric with nervous concern.) So was there a funeral ... for Stephen?
ERIC. No. Just a memorial down in Florida where his parents live.
ALEX. Did you meet them?
ERIC. No. Only his girlfriend ... well, girl-friend. From the band. She came by and got most of his stuff. That was bad enough. I can't even imagine what his parents must be going through.
ALEX. My parents were completely freaked out by all of this ... and I lived! Every time I talk to them on the phone now, they say I love you and are crying. I mean, I love them and everything but it's too much, you know?
ERIC. Oh yeah — it's like people getting all emotional gets me more emotional than I would ever get. It's like this sick cycle.
ALEX. Sick?
ERIC. Well ... yeah. On the 11th, I was managing a sort of thin veneer of sanity. But then Will got here and he acted surprised that I was alive and that was it ... I was gone.
ALEX. Whattya mean?
ERIC. I thought that I wasn't ever gonna stop crying.
ALEX. Like tonight ...
ERIC. Worse actually.
ALEX. Is that possible?
ERIC. Uh ... yeah, unfortunately. It was terrible. I went through half a roll of paper towels. Will just held me and handed me new paper towels and then, during an emotional lull, said that he was taking me to Brooklyn whether I wanted to go or not.
ALEX. Wow — he sounds like a great guy.
ERIC. He has his moments.
ALEX. I mean, it sounds like you really care about him still. Maybe that's why you were crying so much.
ERIC. I don't know ... maybe. It's complicated. It's like that weekend before the 11th, I was just starting to enjoy the idea of really hating Will, in that sorta post-breakup mood you get in. You know, getting really angry at him for everything that had gone wrong in the relationship and it felt soooo good. And then this happened. And now ... I dunno. It's just so damn confusing ... *(Eric is teary-eyed but not crying. Alex looks away and stands up again.)*
ALEX. I'm gonna get back to bed ... wanna join me?
ERIC. And watch you sleep? *(Alex moves closer to him, maybe touching his shoulder, massaging it a little.)*

ALEX. No. We'll both sleep. Together. I'll hold you and help you sleep. It'll be … you know, cozy.
ERIC. I'll just keep you awake. Really. Talking and tossing and … being generally annoying.
ALEX. You're not annoying. You're cute.
ERIC. Thanks.
ALEX. That's why I kissed you in the first place. *(Alex gets up and takes his hand. They start to cross towards the door.)*
ERIC. Not to get me to stop crying.
ALEX. No … *(In the distance, a low menacing rumble can be heard. Eric stops in his tracks.)*
ERIC. Wait a sec —
ALEX. What —
ERIC. F-15s. Maybe something's going on …
ALEX. Like what … *(Eric goes over and clicks on the radio. A song like Bon Jovi's "Living on A Prayer" plays.* The jet rumble gets louder.)*
ERIC. Routine patrol. If it was an attack they wouldn't be playing this song.
ALEX. Unless the DJ had a strange sense of humor. *(Eric looks at him and laughs. Alex laughs and they dissolve into a sort of hysterically contagious laugh. The jets approach overhead, the sound becoming deafeningly loud. The laughter subsides as Eric starts to look a little panicky. He grabs Alex and holds him tightly, clinging onto him for dear life almost. The jets pass over and the noise starts to fade. By the time the noise subsides, Eric is still holding on tight and shaking slightly. Alex seems a little freaked.)* Uh Eric …
ERIC. Yeah.
ALEX. I can't breathe. *(Eric releases Alex from his grasp. Eric, suddenly seems anxious and grabs for a pack of cigarettes. He starts to smoke a bit furiously.)*
ERIC. You want one?
ALEX. No thanks.
ERIC. I'm trying to quit.
ALEX. You know, smoking will keep you up all night. The nicotine is a total stimulant.
ERIC. Yeah … well … you think I'm gonna get any sleep with the Air Force on patrol?
ALEX. Guess not … *(Alex looks exasperated. There's not much more*

---

* See Special Note on Songs and Recordings on copyright page.

58

he can do here to relieve Eric's pain. He sees his pants on the floor and goes to get them and put them on.)
ERIC. What — what're you doing?
ALEX. I'm gonna head out then.
ERIC. Really? It's so late …
ALEX. I've gotta get to work pretty early.
ERIC. You can sleep … have the whole bed to yourself. And I'll make sure you get up. I'll set my alarm. And I can make breakfast. There's coffee and eggs and juice and —
ALEX. Thanks. But I've gotta pick up some papers at home before I go into the office.
ERIC. Where are you staying now anyway?
ALEX. I'm at my parents' house. Way out in Queens.
ERIC. Wow — really?
ALEX. It's just for a few weeks, until I find a share, something more affordable. I wanna save up some money now, get back to school maybe, do something a little more interesting with my life than international bonds, you know.
ERIC. Sounds like a plan. *(Sitting, Alex puts on his shoes.)* Oh — what about the apartment?
ALEX. *(Laughing, he almost forgot.)* Oh yeah … I don't know. I think moving in's probably not a great idea, huh?
ERIC. You sure? I mean, I think we got along pretty well.
ALEX. A little too well … *(A beat.)* Isn't there some rule about not sleeping with your roommate?
ERIC. Technically. But the rules have been suspended due to recent events.
ALEX. Not funny.
ERIC. Not even a little? *(Alex gets up and starts to head to the door. Eric stands.)* Alex?
ALEX. Yeah?
ERIC. Thanks. For staying when I was —
ALEX. Sure.
ERIC. I really needed … and I just … uh, thanks. *(Eric turns around and goes back to the window.)*
ALEX. Take care, Eric. And get some sleep …
ERIC. Maybe a little later. *(Blackout.)*

Scene 8

In darkness, the machine is heard.

ANSWERING MACHINE. Friday, 11:02 A.M.
WILL. *(Voiceover.)* Hey — me again. Just tried your studio but you're not there. Where are you? I wanted to stop by about that dresser, though I'm still not convinced it's not ugly, but also ... I'm a little concerned you haven't called me back since Tuesday. So call me. Or at least send me an email. OK — bye!
ANSWERING MACHINE. Friday, 1:22 P.M.
JOSIE. *(Voiceover.)* OK — so what is the deal with screening calls today? I wanna know what the hell happened with that porn guy. I hope he's not moving in because that would pretty much be a mistake. And I know that I don't even know the guy, but look — you don't want some pervert as a roommate. I mean gay is one thing but — OK, that was a joke. But you're not fucking picking up to laugh at it. Are you in the Bell Jar again? Call me, Eric. Now. *(Lights up on stage. The cardboard boxes are now closed and Eric sits next to one of them, taping it up. He is wearing his T-shirt again. There is a super-sized grande Starbucks on one of the boxes that he picks up and sips from, his J. Crew shirt on a box next to it. There are a couple other empty Starbucks containers on the floor. Eric seems visibly agitated by the message. And probably a bit wired on caffeine.)*
ANSWERING MACHINE. Friday, 3:38 P.M.
LORENZO. *(Voiceover.)* 'Allo — this is Lorenzo. I saw ad in the *Voice* and I'm sorry I didn't call sooner but after the bombing and all I forget. So I like very much but is maybe too expensive. Can we make it less money, maybe 700?
ERIC. *(Overlapping message.)* Now they're bargaining? He's fuckin' crazy ... 700 dollars?!
LORENZO. *(Voiceover.)* I don't think that is too less. I am trying to save money now everything is so bad. I hear from you. Ciao!
ANSWERING MACHINE. Friday, 4:18 P.M.
JEFF. *(Voiceover.)* Hi — Jeff here. Thanks for showing me your

place Wednesday. Unfortunately, we got some new polling in today which was really bad and I just found out that I'm gonna be laid off from the Green campaign. They're having another change in strategy and I'm not part of the change which sucks so I'm going back to Washington. *(Eric reacts strongly to this news by throwing the tape against the wall.)*

ERIC. Fuck! *(Eric stands up and runs his hand through his hair, anxious and frustrated. He starts kicking the box that he has just taped up, it turns over, he kicks it again, stuff falls out, he makes a hole in the side.)* Fuckin' fuck fuck — FUCK!

JEFF. *(Voiceover.)* It's really too bad because it's a great apartment and you seem like a decent normal guy. Anyway, remember to vote for Green — again. Thanks! *(Exhausted, Eric sits on the floor and drops his head with a major sigh. The door buzzer goes off and Eric is jolted by the sound. He yells at the intercom across the room.)*

ERIC. Go away! *(The door buzzer goes off two more times.)* Fuck. *(Eric gets up and goes to the buzzer. He hits the button.)* What.

MAX. *(Offstage.)* Hi — It's Max! From Rainbow Roommates! I'm here to see the —

ERIC. Alright, alright. *(Eric buzzes him in and mutters and mumbles to himself.)* Rainbow fucking Roommates. Bunch of friggin' elves or munchkins dancing around a goddamn real estate pot of gold … *(The door opens offstage and Max enters. He is a cute college student with a bouncy perk in his step. He walks without his heels touching the ground.)*

MAX. Hey — what's up?

ERIC. Just packing up some boxes.

MAX. Oh — making room for me, huh? *(Max, clueless to Eric's angry mood, smiles. Eric glares at him as he strides around the room, checking it out.)* Great place … nice. *(Going towards the window.)* Wow — lots of light.

ERIC. It's only one window.

MAX. Nice view.

ERIC. *(Re: the view.)* Not smoking today?

MAX. You smoke?

ERIC. *(Defiant.)* Yeah. I smoke.

MAX. You should really quit. There's rat poison in those things … I saw it on MTV.

ERIC. *(Oh brother.)* So — what are you, a freshman or something?

MAX. Just started my junior year at NYU.

ERIC. I went to NYU.
MAX. Nice. What'd you study?
ERIC. Photography.
MAX. Oh cool — I love photography.
ERIC. Does anyone hate photography?
MAX. You know, I've been thinking about changing my major. It would be pretty cool, you know. I've always liked pictures. There's this gallery on Spring Street that has all these pictures up from the 11th ... snapshots that people took. It's insane ... so many pictures ... *(A beat.)* Hey — did you take a lot of pictures on the 11th?
ERIC. Uh ... no.
MAX. I got some insane shots on my digital camera. I'll have to show them to you.
ERIC. Uh ... no thanks.
MAX. Then later that day, me and my roommates went up to Union Square. Got some insane pictures there too. We were lighting candles and meditating. It was pretty intense.
ERIC. *(Sarcastic.)* Ohhhh — you were part of that whole 60s love-in thing? *(Max is a little offended by this.)*
MAX. Hey — that's a bit harsh.
ERIC. C'mon ... it was a bunch of students whose classes were cancelled and didn't have anything better to do, right?
MAX. They did cancel class but ...
ERIC. Exactly.
MAX. Man ... why doesn't anyone ever take students seriously? Just because we're young, it's like our opinion is retarded or something. It didn't used to be like this. I took this class last semester, "Remembering the 60s" —
ERIC. They have a class?!
MAX. Oh yeah! People used to listen to students back then. They stopped a war, ended discrimination. Changed everything. Now people look at students and are like — what do they have to say. I think we have a lot to say — no more war and tons more peace.
ERIC. That's just great.
MAX. It is great. It could be. But Bush wants our pain to be a cry for revenge.
ERIC. A little revenge could be a good thing right now.
MAX. *(Totally horrified.)* You're not serious, are you?
ERIC. Look — I wouldn't mind kicking someone's ass for this, OK.

MAX. You have a lot of rage, you know that?

ERIC. Yeah — and why shouldn't I? Thousands of people are dead and someone needs their ass kicked for that. I don't think that's so terrible. It's justice. Simple justice.

MAX. That's what Osama thought.

ERIC. What!?

MAX. He saw his actions as justice for the thousands who have been oppressed and killed by western imperialism in the Middle East. So if we do the same, we're just as bad as he is. Probably worse because we should be setting the example.

ERIC. Your views are really very sweet, Max. But in the real world, peace is an ideal. It's not a way of life.

MAX. Not if you don't think so. It all starts with one person, you know.

ERIC. So you really think that you and your friends gathering together in Union Square are gonna cause an about-face in U.S. foreign policy?

MAX. Maybe not tomorrow but over time.

ERIC. Well … that's great. You know what … you must be in some sort of serious post-everything denial because … I mean, that's … that's just crazy.

MAX. I'd rather be crazy than cynical.

ERIC. I'm not cynical. I'm just realistic.

MAX. Realistic would be realizing your power to change things.

ERIC. Are you in some sort of a cult?

MAX. *(Laughing.)* No way, man.

ERIC. OK — are you from California?

MAX. Nope. Oregon.

ERIC. Oh my god. Even worse!

MAX. It was a great place to grow up, actually. Very progressive and positive energy that — *(Eric walks away from him and towards the door.)* Where you going?

ERIC. I'm sorry, Max. I don't think this is gonna work out.

MAX. What — you mean the apartment thing?

ERIC. I think I just need someone … closer to my … experiences.

MAX. Whattya mean?

ERIC. Someone … just more like …

MAX. Not a student? *(Eric looks at him indicating yes. Max is absolutely deflated.)*

ERIC. Look — there's tons of apartments out there. And tons of

other students too. I'm sure you'll find someone that's, you know, more compatible.
MAX. Man, I shoulda kept my mouth shut about the peace stuff. It drives my roommates crazy.
ERIC. If you have roommates, why are you looking for an apartment?
MAX. They're all leaving school. Our suite's breaking up and they're heading home, leaving the city and everything.
ERIC. Right in the middle of the semester?
MAX. Yeah — it's happening all over school. People's parents are panicked and taking them out. And some friends of mine are just, like, freaking out on their own. I was freaking out too, you know. That day was … it was so insane. Seeing the whole thing live — not on TV.
ERIC. *(About to send him off.)* Yeah … well, we all saw it —
MAX. I mean I was walking down Sixth Avenue, heading to my nine o'clock. The first plane buzzed right over me. I looked up because it was so loud and knew something was totally wrong. And then I followed it and saw it go right into the Trade Center. I mean … right into the building. And that thing had flown right over my head … *(A beat.)* This is kinda weird but … last summer I went to check out that movie *Pearl Harbor* with a couple friends of mine. It was totally stupid — Ben Affleck as some flying ace. Gimme a break. But there was this one scene where the Japanese planes are flying past a bunch of kids playing baseball. And I remember thinking how intense that must have been to be one of those kids. To see history flying right over your head … and when I was watching the movie I thought, damn, nothing that serious or historical is ever gonna happen to me. And then, two months later … there I am on Sixth Avenue looking up. *(A heavy beat.)* And now I feel like, I don't know, like I almost wished something like that to happen. I know I didn't really but … it's what I wanted in a way. To be part of history and now I'm in it all the way.
ERIC. Sounds like you feel guilty …
MAX. *(A revelation.)* Maybe … yeah, I guess so. It's like, I probably felt I had to do something positive after having wished for something negative. That's why I went up to Union Square …
ERIC. At least you tried to do something …
MAX. I had to. Otherwise what's the point of staying?
ERIC. Did you think about leaving?
MAX. Oh yeah. My parents were totally losing it. They live out in

the middle of nowhere and they were trying to get me to come home on a frigging bus. To Oregon. And I seriously considered it for a few days. And I cannot even deal with my parents ...
ERIC. And Union Square got you to change your mind?
MAX. Nah ... it was later, when classes started up on the 17th. In my Psych section, a bunch of students told the teacher that it was gonna be their last class, that they were leaving school because of their folks, and our professor got very down about it. He said he understood their parents' concern but he also said something interesting; that we all came here because we wanted to be in New York, we desired this New York experience, craved it almost. Now, he said, New York needed us. And I was like ... wow. Guy's got a point.
ERIC. So you stayed.
MAX. Yeah. But my roommates left. And now I'm sorta stuck. I can't do university housing and I can't afford my own place.
ERIC. Well — you probably can't afford this place then.
MAX. What is it again?
ERIC. *(Hesitating.)* It's ... it's 1200 a month.
MAX. Whoa — seriously.
ERIC. Uh ... yeah.
MAX. That's a total deal, man! I was expecting like 1500. That's what it is on campus 'cause NYU's a total rip, you know. And I could still walk from here. It'd be per — *(Suddenly, the lights in the apartment flicker and then go off.)* Whoa —
ERIC. What the hell?
MAX. The power blow?
ERIC. That's weird. The power never goes out here. Not even in the summer. Maybe something's going on?
MAX. Whattya mean? *(Eric goes over to his clock radio and flicks it on. Nothing.)*
ERIC. The radio's dead.
MAX. *(Duh.)* Well ... yeah. The power's out.
ERIC. I think something's happening ...
MAX. I read something online that they're having some problems with the power downtown. There was a substation or something got destroyed on the 11th and —
ERIC. Do you have a Walkman or anything?
MAX. Uh ... not on me. You wanna listen to some music?
ERIC. No — I want to check the news. I think something's going on.
MAX. What, like an attack or something? *(In the distance one siren*

is heard, then another. Eric's face blanches.)
ERIC. Oh no ... *(Eric rushes towards the window, opens it and leans out to see what's happening.)* How many sirens is that?
MAX. I dunno — maybe two or three ... *(Looking at him.)* Hey — are you alright?
ERIC. Something's going on.
MAX. Whattya you mean?
ERIC. That's a lot of sirens, don't you think?
MAX. I don't think it's anything to worry about.
ERIC. Oh my god — the traffic lights are out!
MAX. Yeah. Power must be out in the whole neighborhood. *(Car honking is heard coming from outside the window.)*
ERIC. They've killed the traffic lights. Oh my god! It's happening again. We've gotta do something!
MAX. Hey ... relax, it's just the power.
ERIC. No — you don't understand. This is it. Probably a ... a ... a chemical attack, but they're killing the power so no one knows what's going on, no one can get the news on the radio so then we'll all run outside and inhale the stuff and be dead in a few minutes. I've gotta close the window! *(Eric races back to the window to close it but it's stuck. Eric mutters to the window, cursing under his breath, trying to get it unstuck. Max looks at him nervously.)*
MAX. Hey — maybe you'd better sit down for a bit. I seriously don't think anything's wrong.
ERIC. How can you say that ... listen to all those sirens! *(A couple more sirens are heard.)*
MAX. Yeah — it's probably the police. They're coming to help — with the traffic and stuff. It's fine.
ERIC. No — that's too many sirens. I've gotta call Will.
MAX. Who's Will? *(Eric races across the room to the phone. Of course, it's not working either. He drops it.)* Hey — easy there.
ERIC. The phone's dead.
MAX. 'Cause the power's out.
ERIC. I know the power's out. They've cut it! This is it ... *(Eric looks like he's hyperventilating now, pacing around the room in circles almost. Max considers something. Then Eric and Max speak the following blocks of dialogue simultaneously.)*
MAX. Look — maybe you should sit down. Take some deep breaths. I think you're having some kinda panic thing. They talked about this in our dorm last week ... just sit down and take some

deep breaths. They told us you just have to breathe and think of peaceful things ... like a stream or a bubbling brook or —
ERIC. I'm not panicking. This is real. I can't call out — everything's dead. He won't be able to get in touch with me. Will's gonna think I'm dead ... or, oh god, maybe he's dead. He works uptown and maybe that's where the sirens are going. They're probably attacking midtown. I've gotta call Will. Wait — do you have a cell phone?
MAX. Are you gonna relax if I give it to you?
ERIC. Uh — sure. Just lemme make one call — *(Max hands Eric the cell phone. He dials furiously. Max looks out the window curiously.)*
MAX. It looks like everything's fine. I mean, it just looks like an electrical problem. The police are directing traffic — *(Eric puts the cell to his ear and listens. What he hears turns his face white with fear. The cell phone drops out of his hand. Max turns around on hearing this.)* Hey man — my phone!
ERIC. Circuits are busy.
MAX. Yeah — I've got crap service.
ERIC. This is just like before. All the circuits were busy. I couldn't get through. Oh god — this is it. It's all happening again. But this time it's gonna be even worse. This time it's — *(Eric unknowingly backs into a cardboard box on which one of the Starbucks cups sits. The cups tips over and spills onto Eric's J. Crew shirt.)* My shirt ... oh my god! *(Eric holds it up and it now has a big coffee stain on it. Eric is absolutely crushed by this.)* Fuck — Jesus — dammit ...
MAX. Shit ... I mean, you can get another shirt.
ERIC. It was from J. Crew.
MAX. There's J. Crews, like, everywhere.
ERIC. No — I bought it at J. Crew in the mall.
MAX. Yeah ... still. It's okay — you can get a new one.
ERIC. No — J. Crew is gone! It was the one at the Trade Center. And this was the last thing I bought there. And now it's ruined ... totally ruined. *(Eric falls back onto the floor and starts crying again. Max doesn't know what to do.)*
MAX. C'mon, it's just a shirt. *(Eric is sobbing now.)* Oh, man — What's going on? *(The lights and power come back on.)* See — it was just the power. No big deal. *(Looking up, Eric sees this but it makes him even more inconsolable.)* Hey man ... it's fine. See. Everything's fine. Really ...
ERIC. I'm not. I'm not ... fine. I'm not fine. *(Blackout.)*

Scene 9

In darkness, the answering machine is heard.

ANSWERING MACHINE. Monday, 11:02 A.M.
WILL. *(Voiceover.)* Hey — it's me. I talked to Josie and she's gonna get there around one to help, after her doctor's appointment. Anyway, I'll come by with the car after work. Call me if there's any — if you need — you know, just call me when you're there. I wanna make sure everything's okay. Alright ... love you. Bye. *(Lights up. The cardboard boxes are all gone now. Only the dresser and the air conditioner remain. There are also a couple of suitcases near the right wall. Josie enters pulling a small suitcase and holding a set of keys. She goes to look out the window.)*
ANSWERING MACHINE. Monday, 1:38 P.M.
MAX. *(Voiceover.)* Hey — it's Max. How's it going? So I got your message last night and that's totally cool about the apartment. And I talked to Carlos too. He seems cool ... for a landlord I guess. I'm gonna come by after class today and get the keys from him. Alright — later! *(The buzzer goes off. Josie crosses the room, buzzes someone in without saying anything and walks to the center of the room, taking a deep breath and composing herself. Eric enters a few moments later. He is wearing decent clothes, his hair not as disheveled, he has shaved and is generally more put together than the previous scenes. He seems surprised to see her standing in the center of the room, looking at him somewhat anxiously. Josie talks to him in an odd manner, not their usually familiarity.)*
JOSIE. Hey —
ERIC. Hi —
JOSIE. *(Tentative.)* So ... how's it going?
ERIC. Good.
JOSIE. Good. You ... feel okay?
ERIC. Oh, please, Josie ...
JOSIE. What?
ERIC. You don't have to talk to me like that.
JOSIE. Like what?

ERIC. Like I'm Blanche Dubois or something. *(Despite herself, Josie laughs and starts talking like Josie.)*
JOSIE. Well Blanche, at least ya look good ... all dressed up.
ERIC. Oh come on ...
JOSIE. You're actually wearing pants that aren't jeans. And you did something to your hair. Aha — you washed it!
ERIC. OK — are you done making fun of my personal grooming habits.
JOSIE. No. You even shaved too.
ERIC. I had to. Will said I was one step away from looking like a homeless person.
JOSIE. Oh — isn't that sweet!
ERIC. Yeah — he has a way with the compliments sometimes.
JOSIE. So how are things over in Brooklyn?
ERIC. Quiet.
JOSIE. That's the suburbs for you.
ERIC. Yeah ...
JOSIE. But you feel better ...
ERIC. Yeah ... a lot better.
JOSIE. Good. And the 800 number?
ERIC. I've pretty much memorized it.
JOSIE. That's great, Eric. Really. *(Eric smiles at her and looks at the suitcases.)* So where's Max, the amazing rescue boy?
ERIC. He had to go meet with some prospective roommates. He's gonna come by later and get the keys from Carlos.
JOSIE. We're not gonna hand over the keys to the kingdom?
ERIC. No — besides he might be a little freaked out having to see me again.
JOSIE. He sounds like quite a kid ... to keep his cool like that when you were losing it. Calling Will and everything.
ERIC. Yeah — I was pretty lucky he was around. I mean if that had happened and I was alone ...
JOSIE. Let's try not to dwell on the ifs, okay?
ERIC. Okay. *(A beat.)* I can't believe I'm leaving. After almost ten years ...
JOSIE. Ten years ...
ERIC. Makes me feel like a loser.
JOSIE. What?
ERIC. This is exactly what they wanted. To scare me into moving away. Funny ... it's just like you said — the point of terrorism ...

JOSIE. Oh now you're listening to what I said.
ERIC. Yeah, but I fell into that trap ... they made me scared.
JOSIE. Trap?! Eric — they killed your roommate. You have a right to be fucking terrified, okay? There's nothing wrong with that.
ERIC. But still ... leaving here after all this time ... almost a decade.
JOSIE. Alright — let's can the fake nostalgia. How many times did I hear you complain about the lack of heat in the winter and the lack of air conditioning in the summer, locks that sometimes worked, roaches the size of my purse —
ERIC. Okay — I get it. But it was my home, you know.
JOSIE. Well ... now you've got a new home. With central air and a front door that locks.
ERIC. Look — staying at Will's is temporary ...
JOSIE. Really?
ERIC. Really. I'm gonna get everything together, my work and emotional stuff, and then decide on what to do once I can decide.
JOSIE. Sure. When you're thinking clearly ...
ERIC. I'm not gonna stay until he gets sick of me and kicks me out or anything.
JOSIE. He's not gonna get sick of you, Eric.
ERIC. I dunno — I can be pretty difficult these days.
JOSIE. I'm sure Will can handle it. He did a pretty good job on the 11th. And this weekend too. *(A beat.)* I know I don't ever say this but I was probably 100% wrong about him when you two broke up.
ERIC. Josie — 100% wrong? Maybe you need to call that 800 number.
JOSIE. Seriously ... Will's a prince in a time drastically short on them. *(A beat. Eric looks at her curiously.)*
ERIC. Hey — so what was this mysterious doctor's appointment Will mentioned?
JOSIE. Oh that — nothing big really.
ERIC. Josie — you never go to the doctor. What's up?
JOSIE. Oh well ... I'm pregnant.
ERIC. *(Astounded.)* What?! You are?! That's ... that's —
JOSIE. Jesus — Eric, I am a woman — it happens.
ERIC. Yeah, but — you weren't even having sex. And David —
JOSIE. Alright — I've been pregnant for a while.
ERIC. You — really?
JOSIE. I missed my period a couple days after the 11th and I thought I was in shock or something but then I couldn't keep down

my morning latte so I got one of those kits at Duane Reade and … the writing was on the stick, as they say.
ERIC. Wait a minute. So you were actually pregnant when David was wanting to procreate?
JOSIE. Uh … well, yeah.
ERIC. Why didn't you tell him?
JOSIE. Honest?
ERIC. Well, I don't want you to lie to me.
JOSIE. *(Hard to admit.)* I didn't know if I was gonna keep it.
ERIC. Josie!
JOSIE. Don't be all shocked. Jesus — we are liberals.
ERIC. But you were gonna have an abortion?!
JOSIE. Eric — you sound like Jerry fucking Falwell. So I thought about it. That's all. Because of what was going on … the idea of bringing a child into this insanity. *(An emotional beat.)* I mean, reading all these awful stories in the paper about mothers who lost their kids … you know, those Portrait things. Every day there were at least three inconsolable mothers. They were absolutely heartbreaking. And the idea of having a kid only to have something like that happen … I just couldn't — *(Josie stops herself mid-sentence before she gets too emotional. Eric moves closer to her.)*
ERIC. So what changed your mind?
JOSIE. You did.
ERIC. Huh?
JOSIE. The night you freaked out I guess I sorta came to my senses, decided I couldn't keep this a secret from David anymore or I'd end up like you.
ERIC. Gee — thanks.
JOSIE. I had to talk about it with him, stop hiding it and just fucking deal with it. So we had a huge discussion and I told David all my concerns, you know, what we were talking about last week, how the world is just an awful place right now. But he said it'll get better … typical David. Mr. Sunshine raining on Ms. Cynical's parade.
ERIC. Wow — so you're really pregnant …
JOSIE. Yep … I went to the doctor today to break the good news to her.
ERIC. And …
JOSIE. She was thrilled.
ERIC. And you …

JOSIE. I guess I'm pretty excited.
ERIC. So I get to be a fake uncle and everything?
JOSIE. Yeah — but this kid's not gonna call you Uncle Mame. That is just retarded, okay?
ERIC. C'mere ... *(Josie approaches Eric somewhat warily and Eric gives her a big and sincere hug. Josie is almost uncomfortable in the hug. As Eric pulls back, Josie is looking at him oddly.)* What?
JOSIE. We never used to hug before.
ERIC. That's 'cause we were New Yorkers.
JOSIE. And what are we now?
ERIC. Losing it? *(The buzzer goes off.)*
JOSIE. Is that Will already?
ERIC. Probably ... he's never one to be late. *(Eric hits the buzzer.)* Yeah —
WILL. *(Offstage.)* Hey — it's me, honey.
ERIC. Hi — and don't call me honey.
WILL. *(Offstage.)* Sorry, sweetie.
ERIC. Uh — OK — we'll be down in a minute. *(Josie picks up a couple suitcases but Eric wanders over to the window for a last look out. Josie sees him looking and approaches him nervously.)*
JOSIE. Still smoking?
ERIC. Yeah — it's kinda white today. Wispy almost.
JOSIE. *(A little nervous.)* Eric ... you okay?
ERIC. I was listening to NPR last night at Will's. They did this really long piece about the beginnings of the Trade Center. Very NPR, right, to talk about that when everyone is talking about the destruction of it. Anyway, did you know they started construction on the towers the year we were born?
JOSIE. 1968?
ERIC. Yeah ... and it took them more than five years to finish it. I remember coming up to visit my aunt out in Brooklyn for Easter and you could see it from her kitchen window on State Street ... each year it was a little bit taller, a little bit more finished. And I kept asking her, can we go up to the top yet? It was like this obsession I had as a kid ... and I just couldn't wait 'til it was done. When I was eight, the observation deck finally opened. So we all took the subway downtown and took the elevator all the way up and you know what ... it was a major disappointment.
JOSIE. It ... it was? *(Eric is now standing next to the A/C unit, leaning on it with one leg as he continues this story.)*

ERIC. The top deck was closed. Too windy. I tried to convince my aunt that they should let us up anyway, that we'd be fine if she just held my hand, that we wouldn't go flying off the top or anything. I wanted to go up on that observation deck so badly. The view inside was okay but I wanted to be up there on the roof ... the top of the world, I kept calling it.
JOSIE. It was an amazing view.
ERIC. I never took it for granted. Every time someone would come to visit me, I'd take them up there. And every time ... it was a wonder. *(He steps up onto the A/C unit.)* Standing on top with only the sound of the wind ... you couldn't hear any of the street noise of the city that high up. Just wind. And if it was clear enough you could see the curvature of the earth. That was something ... *(A beat.)* Why is it ... why does this thing ... I mean, it was just a building, right?
JOSIE. Apparently not. *(Josie offers a hand to bring him back down to the floor.)* C'mon. Will's waiting ... *(Eric takes her hand and steps off the A/C unit. Josie starts to cross towards the door with Eric behind her but he stops.)*
ERIC. Can I — I'll meet you down there in a sec.
JOSIE. Sure. But if it's more than a minute, I'm calling 911.
ERIC. Okay. Thanks, Josie.
JOSIE. For what?
ERIC. For being Josie.
JOSIE. You've got one minute. *(Josie smiles warmly, nods and leaves the room. Eric looks around at the room and goes to the window as the street noises get louder — buses, cars, honking. He takes the flag down and sticks it in his pocket. He picks up his bags and goes to the door. Just as he's about to leave, he pauses for a moment in the doorway and takes one last look at the room.)*
ERIC. Bye ... *(Eric exits through the doorway on stage right. The lights in the room begin to fade as the street noises get louder, more cacophonous. Finally, the last light dims on the window.)*

End of Play

PROPERTY LIST

3–4 cardboard packing boxes (1 open with clothes, books, cookware, etc.)
Cigarettes, lighter, ashtray
Can of air freshener
Notepad
Pen
Bags of take-out
2 Diet Cokes
Surgical mask
Palm Pilot
Blackberry
Brown paper bag with cupcakes
Cordless phone
Coffee cups
Magazine
Travel mug of coffee
Clock radio
Tape
Large Starbucks cups
Cell phone
Suitcase, keys

SOUND EFFECTS

Medley of sirens
Door buzzer
Honking
Phone rings
Fighter planes

NEW PLAYS

★ **YELLOW FACE by David Henry Hwang.** Asian-American playwright DHH leads a protest against the casting of Jonathan Pryce as the Eurasian pimp in the original Broadway production of *Miss Saigon*, condemning the practice as "yellowface." The lines between truth and fiction blur with hilarious and moving results in this unreliable memoir. "A pungent play of ideas with a big heart." –*Variety.* "Fabulously inventive." –*The New Yorker.* [5M, 2W] ISBN: 978-0-8222-2301-6

★ **33 VARIATIONS by Moisés Kaufmann.** A mother coming to terms with her daughter. A composer coming to terms with his genius. And, even though they're separated by 200 years, these two people share an obsession that might, even just for a moment, make time stand still. "A compellingly original and thoroughly watchable play for today." –*Talkin' Broadway.* [4M, 4W] ISBN: 978-0-8222-2392-4

★ **BOOM by Peter Sinn Nachtrieb.** A grad student's online personal ad lures a mysterious journalism student to his subterranean research lab. But when a major catastrophic event strikes the planet, their date takes on evolutionary significance and the fate of humanity hangs in the balance. "Darkly funny dialogue." –*NY Times.* "Literate, coarse, thoughtful, sweet, scabrously inappropriate." –*Washington City Paper.* [1M, 2W] ISBN: 978-0-8222-2370-2

★ **LOVE, LOSS AND WHAT I WORE by Nora Ephron and Delia Ephron, based on the book by Ilene Beckerman.** A play of monologues and ensemble pieces about women, clothes and memory covering all the important subjects—mothers, prom dresses, mothers, buying bras, mothers, hating purses and why we only wear black. "Funny, compelling." –*NY Times.* "So funny and so powerful." –*WowOwow.com.* [5W] ISBN: 978-0-8222-2355-9

★ **CIRCLE MIRROR TRANSFORMATION by Annie Baker.** When four lost New Englanders enrolled in Marty's community center drama class experiment with harmless games, hearts are quietly torn apart, and tiny wars of epic proportions are waged and won. "Absorbing, unblinking and sharply funny." –*NY Times.* [2M, 3W] ISBN: 978-0-8222-2445-7

★ **BROKE-OLOGY by Nathan Louis Jackson.** The King family has weathered the hardships of life and survived with their love for each other intact. But when two brothers are called home to take care of their father, they find themselves strangely at odds. "Engaging dialogue." –*TheaterMania.com.* "Assured, bighearted." –*Time Out.* [3M, 1W] ISBN: 978-0-8222-2428-0

DRAMATISTS PLAY SERVICE, INC.
440 Park Avenue South, New York, NY 10016 212-683-8960 Fax 212-213-1539
postmaster@dramatists.com www.dramatists.com

NEW PLAYS

★ **A CIVIL WAR CHRISTMAS: AN AMERICAN MUSICAL CELEBRATION by Paula Vogel, music by Daryl Waters.** It's 1864, and Washington, D.C. is settling down to the coldest Christmas Eve in years. Intertwining many lives, this musical shows us that the gladness of one's heart is the best gift of all. "Boldly inventive theater, warm and affecting." *–Talkin' Broadway.* "Crisp strokes of dialogue." *–NY Times.* [12M, 5W] ISBN: 978-0-8222-2361-0

★ **SPEECH & DEBATE by Stephen Karam.** Three teenage misfits in Salem, Oregon discover they are linked by a sex scandal that's rocked their town. "Savvy comedy." *–Variety.* "Hilarious, cliché-free, and immensely entertaining." *–NY Times.* "A strong, rangy play." *–NY Newsday.* [2M, 2W] ISBN: 978-0-8222-2286-6

★ **DIVIDING THE ESTATE by Horton Foote.** Matriarch Stella Gordon is determined not to divide her 100-year-old Texas estate, despite her family's declining wealth and the looming financial crisis. But her three children have another plan. "Goes for laughs and succeeds." *–NY Daily News.* "The theatrical equivalent of a page-turner." *–Bloomberg.com.* [4M, 9W] ISBN: 978-0-8222-2398-6

★ **WHY TORTURE IS WRONG, AND THE PEOPLE WHO LOVE THEM by Christopher Durang.** Christopher Durang turns political humor upside down with this raucous and provocative satire about America's growing homeland "insecurity." "A smashing new play." *–NY Observer.* "You may laugh yourself silly." *–Bloomberg News.* [4M, 3W] ISBN: 978-0-8222-2401-3

★ **FIFTY WORDS by Michael Weller.** While their nine-year-old son is away for the night on his first sleepover, Adam and Jan have an evening alone together, beginning a suspenseful nightlong roller-coaster ride of revelation, rancor, passion and humor. "Mr. Weller is a bold and productive dramatist." *–NY Times.* [1M, 1W] ISBN: 978-0-8222-2348-1

★ **BECKY'S NEW CAR by Steven Dietz.** Becky Foster is caught in middle age, middle management and in a middling marriage—with no prospects for change on the horizon. Then one night a socially inept and grief-struck millionaire stumbles into the car dealership where Becky works. "Gently and consistently funny." *–Variety.* "Perfect blend of hilarious comedy and substantial weight." *–Broadway Hour.* [4M, 3W] ISBN: 978-0-8222-2393-1

DRAMATISTS PLAY SERVICE, INC.
440 Park Avenue South, New York, NY 10016   212-683-8960   Fax 212-213-1539
postmaster@dramatists.com   www.dramatists.com

NEW PLAYS

★ **AT HOME AT THE ZOO by Edward Albee.** Edward Albee delves deeper into his play THE ZOO STORY by adding a first act, HOMELIFE, which precedes Peter's fateful meeting with Jerry on a park bench in Central Park. "An essential and heartening experience." –*NY Times.* "Darkly comic and thrilling." –*Time Out.* "Genuinely fascinating." –*Journal News.* [2M, 1W] ISBN: 978-0-8222-2317-7

★ **PASSING STRANGE book and lyrics by Stew, music by Stew and Heidi Rodewald, created in collaboration with Annie Dorsen.** A daring musical about a young bohemian that takes you from black middle-class America to Amsterdam, Berlin and beyond on a journey towards personal and artistic authenticity. "Fresh, exuberant, bracingly inventive, bitingly funny, and full of heart." –*NY Times.* "The freshest musical in town!" –*Wall Street Journal.* "Excellent songs and a vulnerable heart." –*Variety.* [4M, 3W] ISBN: 978-0-8222-2400-6

★ **REASONS TO BE PRETTY by Neil LaBute.** Greg really, truly adores his girlfriend, Steph. Unfortunately, he also thinks she has a few physical imperfections, and when he mentions them, all hell breaks loose. "Tight, tense and emotionally true." –*Time Magazine.* "Lively and compulsively watchable." –*The Record.* [2M, 2W] ISBN: 978-0-8222-2394-8

★ **OPUS by Michael Hollinger.** With only a few days to rehearse a grueling Beethoven masterpiece, a world-class string quartet struggles to prepare their highest-profile performance ever—a televised ceremony at the White House. "Intimate, intense and profoundly moving." –*Time Out.* "Worthy of scores of bravissimos." –*BroadwayWorld.com.* [4M, 1W] ISBN: 978-0-8222-2363-4

★ **BECKY SHAW by Gina Gionfriddo.** When an evening calculated to bring happiness takes a dark turn, crisis and comedy ensue in this wickedly funny play that asks what we owe the people we love and the strangers who land on our doorstep. "As engrossing as it is ferociously funny." –*NY Times.* "Gionfriddo is some kind of genius." –*Variety.* [2M, 3W] ISBN: 978-0-8222-2402-0

★ **KICKING A DEAD HORSE by Sam Shepard.** Hobart Struther's horse has just dropped dead. In an eighty-minute monologue, he discusses what path brought him here in the first place, the fate of his marriage, his career, politics and eventually the nature of the universe. "Deeply instinctual and intuitive." –*NY Times.* "The brilliance is in the infinite reverberations Shepard extracts from his simple metaphor." –*TheaterMania.* [1M, 1W] ISBN: 978-0-8222-2336-8

DRAMATISTS PLAY SERVICE, INC.
440 Park Avenue South, New York, NY 10016 212-683-8960 Fax 212-213-1539
postmaster@dramatists.com   www.dramatists.com

NEW PLAYS

★ **AUGUST: OSAGE COUNTY by Tracy Letts.** WINNER OF THE 2008 PULITZER PRIZE AND TONY AWARD. When the large Weston family reunites after Dad disappears, their Oklahoma homestead explodes in a maelstrom of repressed truths and unsettling secrets. "Fiercely funny and bitingly sad." –*NY Times.* "Ferociously entertaining." –*Variety.* "A hugely ambitious, highly combustible saga." –*NY Daily News.* [6M, 7W] ISBN: 978-0-8222-2300-9

★ **RUINED by Lynn Nottage.** WINNER OF THE 2009 PULITZER PRIZE. Set in a small mining town in Democratic Republic of Congo, RUINED is a haunting, probing work about the resilience of the human spirit during times of war. "A full-immersion drama of shocking complexity and moral ambiguity." –*Variety.* "Sincere, passionate, courageous." –*Chicago Tribune.* [8M, 4W] ISBN: 978-0-8222-2390-0

★ **GOD OF CARNAGE by Yasmina Reza, translated by Christopher Hampton.** WINNER OF THE 2009 TONY AWARD. A playground altercation between boys brings together their Brooklyn parents, leaving the couples in tatters as the rum flows and tensions explode. "Satisfyingly primitive entertainment." –*NY Times.* "Elegant, acerbic, entertainingly fueled on pure bile." –*Variety.* [2M, 2W] ISBN: 978-0-8222-2399-3

★ **THE SEAFARER by Conor McPherson.** Sharky has returned to Dublin to look after his irascible, aging brother. Old drinking buddies Ivan and Nicky are holed up at the house too, hoping to play some cards. But with the arrival of a stranger from the distant past, the stakes are raised ever higher. "Dark and enthralling Christmas fable." –*NY Times.* "A timeless classic." –*Hollywood Reporter.* [5M] ISBN: 978-0-8222-2284-2

★ **THE NEW CENTURY by Paul Rudnick.** When the playwright is Paul Rudnick, expectations are geared for a play both hilarious and smart, and this provocative and outrageous comedy is no exception. "The one-liners fly like rockets." –*NY Times.* "The funniest playwright around." –*Journal News.* [2M, 3W] ISBN: 978-0-8222-2315-3

★ **SHIPWRECKED! AN ENTERTAINMENT—THE AMAZING ADVENTURES OF LOUIS DE ROUGEMONT (AS TOLD BY HIMSELF) by Donald Margulies.** The amazing story of bravery, survival and celebrity that left nineteenth-century England spellbound. Dare to be whisked away. "A deft, literate narrative." –*LA Times.* "Springs to life like a theatrical pop-up book." –*NY Times.* [2M, 1W] ISBN: 978-0-8222-2341-2

DRAMATISTS PLAY SERVICE, INC.
440 Park Avenue South, New York, NY 10016 212-683-8960 Fax 212-213-1539
postmaster@dramatists.com www.dramatists.com